TO BOB

TRust You ENJOY THE stoRy

LOVE

MICHAEL

We Must Forgive to Live

<small>MICHAEL PARLEE</small>

authorHOUSE®

AuthorHouse™ LLC
1663 Liberty Drive
Bloomington, IN 47403
www.authorhouse.com
Phone: 1-800-839-8640

Published by AuthorHouse   12/09/2013

ISBN: 978-1-4918-3033-8 (sc)
ISBN: 978-1-4918-3032-1 (hc)
ISBN: 978-1-4918-3031-4 (e)

Library of Congress Control Number: 2013919551

DEDICATION

This book is dedicated to all those who are struggling with the pain that the injustices of life have brought their way. It is my hope that they, like the author, will find the peace, tranquillity and wholeness that only the granting of forgiveness can bring.

ACKNOWLEDGMENTS

As with my other two books I would like to acknowledge and thank my editor, Barb Baer, and my wife, Pauline, for their support, advice and encouragement. 'We Must Forgive to Live' has evolved into a much better book because of their help.

Introduction

WE MUST FORGIVE TO LIVE

In early January of 1933, Ukraine was under the heel of the Russia communist party. Bringing collective farming into rural Ukraine was being met with stiff resistance from the land-owner farmers. In a show of force, to bring the rural population into line, Stalin's government initiated mass deportations, executions and most macabre of all, a man-made famine.

Although the Ukraine was the bread basket of the Russian empire, the Russians confiscated most of the food the farmers produced. They were literally starving the farmers in an attempt to force them onto collective farm communes. The large stockpiles of grain throughout the rural areas were destined for export and guarded by the army. Anyone caught trying to take grain from these stockpiles ran the risk of being shot by the guards. The cruel reality was that before the famine would lift, millions of Ukrainians would die of starvation. Our story begins in the small Ukrainian farming village of Novich, some eighty kilometres east of the Polish border.

CHAPTER 1

The early winter twilight was descending on the village of Novich in western Ukraine. All was silent save for the weak cries of the sunken-cheeked, starving children. It would be another cold night. The north wind whisked away the smoke from the chimneys. In the distance one could hear the mournful howling of a starving dog. It would no doubt succumb to starvation before sunrise.

In the Goodz household, little eighteen-month old Elena had cried almost all her waking hours for the last two months.

Starvation had drastically changed her. Once she was a bright-eyed, chubby, cheerful, robust little being. Now Elena's stomach protruded and her arms and legs looked like broomsticks. As long as they would live, her parents and older brother would be haunted by her sorrowful never-ending crying. Maria, her mother, breastfed Elena, but because of next to nothing to eat, Maria's milk supply had long since dried up. The last few days, the crying had changed to a barely audible whimper.

Even though it was prohibited by the Russian army, the Goodz's had managed to hide a small stockpile of food in a secret compartment in their cellar, but that small cache had been used up long ago. Maria held her dying baby close, slowly rocking her, tears slipping down her sunken cheeks.

Before the famine ravished her body, Maria was a striking beauty. She had blue eyes, was fair skinned and her hair was the colour of ripe wheat straw. She had been just a little on the plump side.

"Hospodeh Pomiloy, Hospodeh Pomiloy. (God have mercy, God have mercy,)" she chanted over and over again. By Maria's side sat Roger, her emaciated nine year old son. His legs and arms were spindly, his stomach bloated. He looked on, despair and fear playing across his thin ashen face.

"I'm so hungry Mama. Isn't there anything to eat?" he kept saying.

"I'm sorry, Son, but we'll have to wait until your tato comes home," was Maria's constant reply. "He usually finds something to eat. It's the Russian Government that's to blame. God will help us. Try to be brave."

Gregory, Roger's dad, had been gone since noon, desperately searching for a little something to feed his starving family. It was now dark as he slowly pushed open the door into their small white-washed kitchen.

Gregory was swarthy. His once stocky, husky frame was reduced to a frail shadow of its old self. Only the gnawing hunger and a passion to feed his starving family kept him going.

"Thank God we had a little luck," he began, placing a small chunk of frozen meat on the kitchen table. "Stefan and I found the spot where the Russians took some of the dead horses. It was just a kilometre out of town. Someone else must have got there first because we found part of a hind quarter away from the pit where the dead horses were placed. Stefan and I managed to salvage a little bit of meat. It's still frozen. It looked like the horses hadn't been there that long."

While Gregory held Elena, Maria shaved the frozen horsemeat into thin slices and fried it. Once the meat was cooked they dug in. It wasn't very savoury, but they gobbled it down, hardly taking time to chew. Gregory carefully made sure that Maria and Roger had most of their meagre supper.

"I'll see if I can get Elena to eat a little," Maria said, her voice breaking. "She's so weak. God alone knows how much longer she can hold on."

Maria chewed up some of the meat and tried to get Elena to eat it, but the poor baby was unable to chew. In desperation Maria took a slice and boiled it until it was a soupy mush, but the little tyke was too weak to swallow.

Late into the night, Maria sat rocking her baby, chanting over and over, "Hospodeh Pomiloy, Hospodeh Pomiloy." Gregory and Roger sat close by, silently weeping. Finally, the whimpering stopped. As Maria, Gregory and Roger watched in anguish, the life light slowly faded from Elena's eyes. Her long struggle with hunger was over. The baby girl was free at last.

From the bottom of Maria's soul came a mother's painful cry. "My darling baby's gone, she's gone," Maria wailed. "God help us. God help us."

"My spirit is crushed," Gregory whispered. "There's no use in cursing the Russians anymore. It takes too much energy. The little strength we have left we must save to fight the hunger a bit longer."

Slowly he dropped to his knees and placed his hand on Elena's forehead. "My precious baby, my precious Elena," he cried. "God have mercy, God have mercy."

Roger sat in stunned silence. With tears slipping down his cheeks, he hesitantly placed his hand on his little sister's forehead.

3

"Why did my little sister have to die, Mama?" Roger finally blurted out.

Maria shook her head, but did not reply.

Anticipating Elena's death, Gregory made the baby a small, simple coffin. Maria, with Gregory's help, prepared the tiny body. They put Elena in her red woollen dress and laid the tiny wasted body in the wooden box. Maria placed Elena's doll beside her and tucked her favourite blanket around her. They put the little coffin on a chair beside the bed. For a long time, Maria lay there, weeping and holding her baby's small hand.

"We must try not to be angry with God," she whispered to Gregory and Roger. "If the truth is known, Elena is the lucky one. She's with her Baba and the angels. They'll take good care of her."

Totally spent, Maria finally fell asleep.

Just before daybreak, Maria had a most vivid dream. She was in the garden getting vegetables for dinner. "Mama, Mama!" Maria whirled around. Elena was running toward her, golden hair flying in the breeze. At the back of the garden stood a young woman dressed in white. Elena appeared to be about four years old. "Mama, I'm so happy here. I have lots of kids to play with."

Elena reached her arms up to her mama.

Maria reached down to pick her up, but as suddenly as they had appeared, Elena and the lady in white were gone.

Maria woke Gregory and told him of her dream.

"What a wonderful, wonderful gift," Gregory whispered. "I haven't the slightest doubt that our little girl's spirit came to you to comfort us. If things don't soon get better we will all be with her."

"The dream will be a comfort to me as long as I live," Maria replied.

While he still had the strength, Gregory dug a large shallow grave at the end of the garden. The next morning they placed Elena's little casket in the grave. Gregory, Maria and Roger silently stood by the small mound of dirt for some time. In a breaking voice, Maria began singing, 'Jesus Loves the Little Children.'

In the cold of the dawn, they continued standing in silence, holding hands and weeping.

And so it went, day after day, desperate rural villagers and country folk, fighting starvation with every ounce of strength their weakened bodies possessed.

In the days following Elena's death, the family's physical condition was steadily deteriorating. Like his folks, Roger was getting progressively weaker and now spent most of the day in bed. Gregory's sorties looking for food were getting shorter because of his weakening condition. Some days he'd return with nothing. At noon, after a small bowl of cabbage soup, Gregory and Stefan left to try to scavenge some food.

Maria was apprehensive. She was aware that if the authorities caught you stealing food or hoarding, it could mean execution.

Gregory and Stefan had long past given up on checking where the horses were buried as the burial site was now guarded. Gregory returned in late afternoon with less than a cup of cracked wheat and a small frozen turnip.

"God help us," he wheezed, slumping down at the kitchen table. "I don't know how much longer I can keep looking for food. My strength is just about gone."

As it took some time for the wheat to cook, they couldn't eat until midnight. To conserve energy, they all slept together and didn't get up until ten the following morning.

At noon, Gregory left again to try to find food. He stopped to pick up Stefan, but Stefan was too weak to go.

"If I find some food I'll share it with you as we always do," Gregory said to Stefan and his wife. "I'll check in before dark."

It would be one of Gregory's off days. After two hours of searching, he found absolutely nothing. He was so desperate that he embarked on a dangerous plan. About a kilometre out of the village was a large storage bin holding over one hundred tons of wheat destined for export. Gregory and Stefan thought of trying to take a little grain from the bin before, but fear always dissuaded them. It was guarded around the clock and two men from the village had been shot by the guards last month, attempting to steal wheat.

Gregory decided to wait until dark and then try to sneak up to the backside of the large storage shed. He heard that someone made a small hole in the backside of the bin that was stuffed with an old sock and covered with snow. In the growing darkness, Gregory headed out, trying to stay in the shadows. Because he was so weak, he had to stop several times to rest. Fortunately, clouds obscured the moon. He finally made it to a clump of trees 150 metres from the shed. He waited there until it was completely dark. Slowly and stealthily he crawled up to the bin. He counted the rafters on the roof. Finding the eleventh rafter he sighted down to the ground and began pawing away at the snow.

"Thank God," he whispered, finding the sock. Carefully he scooped the wheat into a small bag, put the sock back in the hole and spread the snow back over it.

His heart began beating wildly as the moon came out from behind a cloud, illuminating the whole country side. Gregory glanced up at the moon and cursed his luck. On hands and knees he began crawling back to the grove. At the edge of the trees he breathed a sigh of relief and stood up.

CRACK! The sound of a gunshot rang out. Gregory did not hear the shot, but felt the stabbing pain in his back.

Suddenly, he was looking down on his body sprawled in the snow. He glanced up to a sight that warmed his whole being. Little Elena and her baba were coming towards him, their arms outreached.

"We have come to take you with us," Baba said, taking Gregory by the hand.

With his other hand in Elena's, Gregory's spirit rose up with them. His long battle with hunger was over. He was going home.

CHAPTER 2

By ten in the evening, Gregory still hadn't returned.

"I hope nothing has happened to Tato," Roger said, his voice very weak. "Shouldn't he be home by now?"

"We'll just have to be patient," Maria replied, desperately trying to hide her panic. "Remember, other times he's been quite late."

After dividing what was left of the turnip, they turned in. Maria had difficulty getting to sleep. She kept it from Roger, but was terrified that Gregory had gotten into trouble. The few times he had been late in the past happened when he was in much better shape. Lately, because he was so weak, he'd only be gone for two or three hours. Maria and Roger woke at eight with a start. Gregory still hadn't returned. Maria was praying constantly for her husband. They waited all morning with growing apprehension.

At two-thirty in the afternoon they heard someone coming up their walk.

"Maybe that's Tato now," Maria said hurrying to the door.

It was Louise, Stefan's wife.

"Stefan is worried sick about Gregory and asked me to see if he had come home last night without stopping at our place. We're both getting so weak. Stefan can hardly walk and he's nearly blind."

"No, he hasn't come home yet," Maria replied, fear playing across her face. "I hope he's okay. It's been over 24 hours since he left."

"God help us all," Louise replied, slumping down in a chair. "You've suffered so much, Maria. You lost Elena and now who knows what's up with Gregory. For years I thought it a curse that Stefan and I couldn't have children, but with this horrible famine, I'm now thinking it's a blessing. When I get home, Stefan and I will pray for Gregory's safe return."

After a cup of weak tea, Louise left.

Maria was Jewish. Her widowed father, Jacob, lived less than a hundred kilometres away in Poland, just a short distance from the border with the Ukraine. Before the Russian army clamped down on all communications out of the Ukraine, Maria sent her dad a letter telling him of the deepening political situation.

Jacob received her letter some time back. Although he was concerned for Maria and her family's welfare, he was unaware how grave the situation had recently become. Then a couple of weeks ago he heard stories of the rural Ukrainians dying of starvation and was becoming increasingly worried for his daughter and her family. He learned that some Ukrainians bought their freedom by bribing the Russian army. He was now hoping to somehow spirit his daughter and her family out of the Ukraine into Poland.

Jacob was a merchant and operated a small general store in Kozmin, a town of 3000. He was in his early sixties. Although fairly tall, he was slight of build. With a mat of white hair and a short beard he looked quite distinguished.

He knew an unsavoury character by the name of Igor Ivonovitch who was making a livelihood bartering with the Russian army that occupied the Ukraine. Igor's father was Russian, his mother Polish. Bribing the Russian army for his Polish clients was his profession.

Via the grapevine, Jacob sent word out that he wanted Igor to stop by his store.

The next day Igor dropped by. Jacob took him into his office and closed the door. Igor passed up the wooden chair provided for him and sprawled out in Jacob's stuffed armchair. Igor was quite overweight, of short stature and slovenly dressed. When he talked, he had a habit of looking past you, seldom making eye contact.

"I am getting very concerned for my daughter and her family," Jacob said. "They live in rural Ukraine and from what I hear many in that area are dying of starvation. Is there any way you could help me bring them here and what would it cost? They have a small farm near the village of Novich, but they live right in the village. Are you familiar with that area?"

"Yes I'm quite familiar with that region. Since the start of the famine I've helped get a number of Ukrainians out of that area. You're right. From what I've been told, many are dying of starvation. Unfortunately, it's getting harder to smuggle anyone out as the Russians now want far bigger bribes. I'll see what I can do though. I know the lieutenant who is in charge of that area. He can be hard to deal with, but I'll do my best. Give me the name of your daughter's family and I will check in with Lieutenant Bodner. I'm headed into the Ukraine tomorrow on other business."

"I'll get back in touch with you as soon as I can. If I can make a deal with the lieutenant, you should be prepared to pay a fairly high price, especially if they find out your daughter is Jewish. You understand, I have nothing against Jews myself," he continued in an oily unconvincing tone. "You know the Russians though. I won't know until I talk to the lieutenant, but you should be prepared to pay something like 2000 Russian roubles in gold. My fee would be another 20% of that."

"I'll suggest to the lieutenant that he use the spot four kilometres north of the Kozmin border crossing. We've used it a number of times before. You may know the spot I'm talking about. There's a large grove of trees there, maybe thirty or forty hectares. The grove straddles the border. In the middle of the grove is a small meadow. That's the rendezvous spot. A trail leads into the meadow from both the Ukrainian and Polish sides."

"Yes I know the spot. Years ago the wife and I used to pick blueberries there."

"If you'd be so kind, I'll need 40 roubles in advance," Igor continued. "Sometimes one has to bribe the guards at the border crossing just to get into the Ukraine."

Jacob handed Igor the money and they shook hands to consummate the deal.

When Igor met with Lieutenant Bodner the next day, the first thing he mentioned was that Maria was Jewish.

Lieutenant Bodner was a big, swarthy, burly man with a drawn, hard face. Those under his command feared his violent temper.

"Tell this Jew that getting his daughter and family out will cost him plenty," the lieutenant roared. "I shouldn't deal with a damn Jew, but then I guess money is money. I want 2400 roubles in gold up front from him. If he accepts my asking price we'll have to get right at it or his daughter and family might starve to death," the lieutenant added with a sadistic grin. "When will you see this Jacob again and when can you get back to me? If he accepts my offer where can I drop them off?"

"I'll be seeing him tonight and I'll be coming back into the Ukraine on other business tomorrow," Igor said. "How about dropping them off at that spot on the border four kilometres north of the Kozmin crossing? We've used it before."

"Good, I'm familiar with that location."

"Four hundred eighty less the 40 Jacob advanced me will make my share 440 in gold," Igor mused as they parted. "Not a bad take for an uneducated Pole."

With the prospect of a payday as big as that, Igor dropped in on Jacob as soon as he returned from the Ukraine.

"As I told you before, the Russians are getting harder to deal with," Igor began. "Lieutenant Bodner demanded to know your daughter's nationality. When he found out she was Jewish, he upped the price to 2400 roubles in gold. He is demanding all the money up front before he allows them to come to Poland."

"That's robbery, but I guess I have no choice. Here's my part of the deal. I'll give him 1200 up front and 1200 when he brings me my daughter and family. That's my one and only offer."

"And for me, as I mentioned before, my fee would be twenty per cent of the 2400, less of course the 40 roubles you gave me in advance," Ivonovich whined. "You must appreciate that I'm in a very risky business with a wife and family to support. I don't think I need to tell you how dangerous it is, especially when I'm in the Ukraine. One slip up and you can get yourself shot. I'll give the lieutenant your counter offer. If he accepts it, I'll be back in touch with you as soon as possible."

Jacob offered Igor 220 roubles in gold as an advance and the other 220 roubles when his daughter and family arrived, but Igor adamantly insisted that his fee be paid him up front. Reluctantly, Jacob gave him his 440 roubles fee plus the 1200 roubles for the Lieutenant.

The next day Igor again met with Lieutenant Bodnar, handed him the 1200 roubles in gold and gave him Jacob's counter offer.

"Damn those Jews anyway," Bodnar stormed, "always bartering. No wonder everyone hates them. I should call the deal off, but as I said before, I guess money is money. How soon can you make contact with this Jacob? We'd better do it tonight if possible."

"I should be able to get back to Kozmin by five this evening. I told Jacob that the rendezvous spot would be the one we've talked about. I told him you'd be at the meeting place with his family tonight or tomorrow night.

"Good. So have this Jacob meet me there at three tomorrow morning. Tell him to be sure he has the other 1200 roubles or no deal."

It was Igor's intent to get the message to Jacob as quickly as possible, but with 400 plus roubles in gold in his pockets it didn't work out quite as planned.

A few kilometres short of Jacob's place, on his return trip, Igor stopped in at the Bolskys with a large bottle of vodka. Like Igor, the Bolskys were an unsavoury bunch, making their livelihood much the same way Igor did, smuggling whatever they could get their hands on across the border. Like Igor, their business was selling their souls to the Russians for the best price they could get.

One thing led to another and they were soon into the vodka with a vengeance. By the time midnight came, Igor had passed out without making contact with Jacob. The whole plan of Maria and Roger escaping the horrors of the famine was now in jeopardy . . . .

Late in the evening, the lieutenant headed to Novich to pick up Maria and her family. He assumed that by now Igor would have made contact with Jacob. When Bonder contacted the officer in charge of the village he was informed that the infant Goodz baby girl had died a few weeks ago and Gregory, the husband had been shot stealing wheat the day before.

The last 24 hours were very heavy for Maria and Roger as Gregory had still not made an appearance. They had nothing to eat and only a little weak tea to drink. They were just getting ready for bed when there was a loud knock at the door. Before Maria could answer it, the door burst open. Maria shook in fear. It was a soldier from the dreaded Russian army. Lieutenant Bodnar decked out in his long great coat was a frightening sight to Maria and Roger.

"You are Maria Goodz and this is your son Roger?" He asked in broken Ukrainian.

"That's right," Maria replied, her voice trembling.

Bodner walked from room to room with his revolver drawn. Satisfied there was no one else in the house, he returned to the kitchen and holstered his gun.

"You and the boy; put on your winter clothes and get your blankets."

"Where are we going?" Maria asked timidly. "What about my husband Gregory? Would you know his whereabouts?"

"Never mind," the lieutenant replied without making eye contact. "Just hurry."

In a few minutes Maria and Roger were dressed in their winter clothes. Bodner took the blankets and led them to the back of the army truck, helped them in and stuffed the blankets in after them. The truck had a canvas-covered back and was very cold. Maria and Roger lay on a foul smelling straw tick and covered themselves with the blankets. While Maria completely covered Roger, she kept her head uncovered, trying to catch any conversation that would clue her in as to their fate.

"Where are we going and what about Tato?" Roger asked, pulling the blankets back.

"I don't know what's happening," Maria whispered as the truck started moving. "We must do as they say. All we can do is pray."

After a few minutes of shivering, they slowly began to warm up. Despite their apprehension and the roughness of the ride, Maria and Roger finally fell into a troubled sleep . . . .

Jacob was expecting Igor sometime in the early evening. By 10 PM he was getting quite worried as Igor hadn't made an appearance. Igor had advised him that should Bonder accept his offer, he could bring his daughter and her family to the rendezvous spot either at 3AM tonight or 3AM tomorrow night.

By midnight, Jacob was getting desperate. Fearing that something had happened to Igor, he decided to take action.

Jacob looked at his watch and reckoned he had about two hours to get to the exchange spot. He made borsch for supper and had a large pot of it on the back of the stove. He took the warm pot of borsch, wrapped it in a blanket and put it in a basket with a loaf of bread and some butter. A team of horses and a cutter was his means of conveyance in the winter. In less than half an hour, he was on his way. As he travelled along the snow-packed road, he was deep in thought.

"Am I on a wild goose chase? Did Igor carry out his part of the deal and give the first 1200 roubles to the lieutenant? How wise was it for me to strike out in the middle of the night on nothing stronger than a hunch?" The closer he got to the proposed rendezvous point, the more he questioned the wisdom of his midnight journey.

He arrived at the meeting place at twenty to three and stopped on the Polish side, fifty meters from the border. It was a moonlit night with the occasional cloud scuttling across the sky.

"I hope this isn't all foolishness," he mused as he sat there waiting. "It may not have been wise to come all this way on just a strange feeling, but something must have happened to Igor. Really, what else could I do?"

By three AM he stepped out of the cutter, hoping to hear or see something. There was nothing to be seen or heard other than the occasional sound coming from the horses. At twenty after three he was about ready to say his trip was all for naught when off in the distance he heard a faint sound. Jacob's heart started beating wildly when he recognized that the sound was an approaching vehicle coming without the lights on.

Lieutenant Bodnar spotted Jacob's cutter on the far side of the meadow and stopped the truck on the Ukrainian side. While the border crossings were manned, the rendezvous point was isolated and protected by tree cover.

With his revolver in hand the lieutenant approached the cutter.

Jacob had been forewarned by Igor that the lieutenant would no doubt be armed as a precaution against an ambush.

Jacob saw him coming and stepped out of the cutter onto the snow.

"Do you speak Russian?" the lieutenant asked in passible Polish.

"Ukrainian, Polish, Russian and German," Jacob replied in flawless Russian.

"Good," Bodnar replied. "We'll use Russian." With his gun drawn he carefully checked the inside of the cutter.

"Igor must have gotten to you then. I'm relieved. I've dealt with him before and he's not to be trusted."

"To be honest with you, he didn't stop," Jacob continued, handing over the bag of gold coins. "He told me that probably the rendezvous place would be here, tonight or tomorrow night at 3 AM. I just got this strange feeling that I should be here tonight."

"I'll be dealing with that bastard rat," the lieutenant growled, putting his revolver back in its holster. "I was leery of trusting him. He's a slimy character."

The lieutenant started to slowly count out the gold coins.

"You have brought my daughter, son-in-law, grandson and infant granddaughter?" Jacob asked when Bodnar finished the count.

"I brought your daughter and grandson," the lieutenant replied icily.

"What about my son-in-law and granddaughter?"

"They were not there."

The lieutenant did not amplify, but the look on his face told Jacob that he knew more.

"Well the amount is right," he said giving a nod. "I'll go get them now."

Jacob stepped back into the cutter.

Maria did not dare look out the back of the truck, but heard the sound of receding footsteps and then the faint sound of men talking. Maria and Roger huddled together terrified of what their fate would be. Then they heard the crunch of footsteps in the snow and the truck's canvas flap was pulled back.

"Get up, take your blankets and follow me," the lieutenant began.

He lifted Roger over the tail gate and then helped Maria out. The lieutenant had to carry the blankets as Maria and Roger were too weak. With apprehension, they slowly followed the soldier.

As they were nearing the cutter, he spoke in Ukrainian. "You are lucky. Your father bought your freedom."

The soldier dropped the blankets beside the cutter and without another word, headed back to his truck.

Jacob stepped out of the cutter.

"Maria," he called out.

"Father," Maria replied weakly.

She fell into her dad's arms and wept. Jacob helped them into the cutter and wrapped their blankets around them. He opened the basket, handed them large soup bowls, slices of buttered bread and then ladled out the borsch.

"I knew you'd be starving so I brought you a pot of borsch and some bread."

"I've never tasted anything so good in all my life," Maria replied between spoonfuls. "Thank God you got us out."

"I see they didn't bring little Elina and Gregory," Jacob continued, after giving them a chance to eat. "I paid the Russian officer to bring the whole family out. What about Gregory and Elena?"

"Elena starved to death about three weeks ago," Maria replied, tears slipping down her cheeks. "As for Gregory, we don't know where he is. Two days ago he went looking for food and didn't return. I fear he got caught by the army."

"My heart goes out to you for the loss of Elena," Jacob replied, putting his arm around his daughter.

"That icy, all-knowing look in Lieutenant Bodner's eyes when I asked him about my son-in-law," Jacob thought. "It doesn't look good for Gregory."

It took close to two hours to reach Jacob's place. Roger stuffed himself with as much borsch and buttered bread as his shrunken stomach could hold. For the first time in months, he felt full. It wasn't long into their return trip before he was asleep.

"Thank you, God, for saving Roger and me," Maria silently prayed as they neared Kozmin. "If he's still alive, please bring our Gregory to us."

CHAPTER 3

It had been a few years since Maria and Roger had been in Kozmin. As Jacob opened the door to the store, the smell of groceries and dry goods brought back fond childhood memories for Maria.

"I had no idea things were so bad or I'd have tried to get you out sooner," Jacob said after hearing of the plight Maria and the family suffered. "From what I hear it's that monster Stalin and his henchmen who are to blame."

"Yes, without question they're monsters all right," Maria replied. "I know for sure that close to a third of our village has starved to death. As with Elena, it's the very young who are suffering most. All our livestock, grain, hay and most of our garden produce was confiscated. Gregory had a feeling that things would get bad so we had a fair amount of food stashed away in a secret compartment he dug into our cellar. Even though we rationed that food, it ran out a long time ago. Ever since then we've been scrounging for anything that a person could eat, dead horses and dogs, even rats. I don't know this for a fact, but there are rumours of cannibalism going on. Since Elena died, we've been getting weaker and weaker. I doubt if we'd have survived another week. I just hope and pray that somehow my Gregory survives."

The day after Jacob picked up Maria and Roger, a very flustered, hung over Igor stopped at the store.

"I'm so glad you have your daughter and grandson here with you," he began without making eye contact. "I was on my way back from seeing the lieutenant when some idiots in the Russian army detained me. They just let me go a few hours ago." Having given his fabricated alibi, Igor beat a hasty retreat.

Over the next few weeks, Maria and Roger were building up their strength. Maria and Jacob marvelled how Roger seemed to eat non-stop. Maria began cooking and housekeeping for Jacob, while Roger started school. Both Maria and Roger worried constantly over Gregory's whereabouts.

"I wonder if we should get a hold of Igor again and try to get some information on Gregory," Jacob said one evening as they were eating supper. "I hate dealing with him because he's such a despicable character, but he has his contacts with the Russian army and seems to have an inside track with them."

"It's worth a try," Maria replied. "I'm desperate to get any kind of information on Gregory, even if it's bad news."

Jacob put out word that he wanted to see Igor and a few days later he turned up at the store.

After some customary haggling, they settled on a fee and the next day Igor was on the road into the Ukraine to get word on Gregory's welfare. Three days later, Igor returned and stopped at the store. Maria and Jacob talked with him in Jacob's office.

"I'm afraid I have bad news about your husband and son-in-law," Igor began. "I had to pay Lieutenant Bodnar a hefty sum just to get into Novitch. He was more difficult to deal with than ever. Anyway, I talked to neighbours of yours, Fred something and his wife. They found out that the evening Gregory did not return he had broken into a government grain storage bin. He was shot dead by a guard as he was trying to make a getaway with a small bag of wheat. The neighbour I talked to, this Fred character asked the army if they could bring the body to the house. He said the army brought the body and Fred and his wife buried him next to his daughter. I'm sorry I couldn't bring you good news. Fred and I went into the house and gathered all the pictures we could find."

Igor handed Maria a small cloth sack.

"That neighbour would be Fred Kowalchuk and his wife Lucy," Maria whispered, tears slipping down her cheeks. "At least Gregory is not suffering anymore. Thanks so much for bringing the pictures. That's all we have of our old life now. They'll mean so much to Roger and me."

For Maria, keeping busy helped lessen the pain. As her strength returned, she was not only looking after the household, but gave her dad a few hours help every day in the store. Soon Roger was helping after school and on Saturdays. Despite the loss of Gregory and Elena; Maria, Roger and Jacob were becoming a close-knit family.

As time passed, Maria was growing more and more concerned over Roger's emotional state. Although he was doing well in school and proved a conscientious worker in the store, his demeanour remained morose and he was not trying to make friends.

"Life's not fair," Roger said one night at the supper table. "All the other kids in my class have dads and brothers and sisters, but I have none. I hate the Russians so much for killing Tato and Elena."

"I'm worried about Roger," Maria said to her father the next morning after Roger left for school. "I know he was very close to his tato, but it's been quite some time since he lost him and Elena. He doesn't seem to be able to get over his loss."

"I'd have to agree with you on that," Jacob replied, shaking his head. "Have you noticed how many hours he spends looking at the photographs that Igor brought you and how sad he looks?"

"Can we talk, Roger?" Maria said one evening as Roger sat at the kitchen table looking at the old family photos.

"I'm so concerned for you, Son. It's been a long time since we left the Ukraine and you're still very sad. Is there anything you'd care to talk about?"

"There's nothing to talk about," Roger responded, wiping his eyes on his sleeve. "I've got no Dad or sister and I'll never get them back. I hate those Russians something awful."

Maria shook her head and went back to drying the dishes.

Maria continued to spend countless hours talking to her son with the hope of bringing him out of his shell. She was earnestly prayed that time would lessen the sting. Nothing she did seemed to help. Finally, in desperation, she approached her Rabbi.

"I'm so concerned for my son," she began. "He seems hopelessly stuck over the deaths of his tato and sister. I've done everything I can for him, but it's not working."

"You've mentioned the young lad's problem before. If you think it would help, I could talk to him. Next week I'm teaching a class on religion in the school. It's the last class of the day. Perhaps after the class I could meet with him."

"Your mother told me a bit of your family and the loss of your dad and sister," the Rabbi began when he and Roger were alone after class. "Let's talk a bit about your feelings."

"I really don't want to talk about it," Roger blurted out. "What's there to say? Mom's always going on about it with me. I hate the Russians for killing my family and there's nothing more to say."

Realizing it would be fruitless to talk any more about Roger's losses, the Rabbi quickly changed the subject.

"I met with Roger after school," the Rabbi said when he next met Maria. "From my perspective, he's unable to climb out from under the pain of his loss. Then again, it's been close to two years since you and he arrived, so on second thought, maybe we should change that 'unable' to 'unwilling.' Without question, time isn't doing much to lessen the pain for the lad. I've observed that there are some people who make a concerted effort to stay stuck in their grief."

"Until Roger is willing to move on, there is not much we can do for the young fellow. I know you've spent a lot of time trying to get him back on his feet. All we can do is hope and pray he'll soon get a handle on his life."

Six months later, Maria's and the Rabbi's hopes for Roger seemed to be coming to fruition. Roger had started a friendship with Emil, a Jewish boy from the Ukraine. Emil, like Roger, had escaped the famine with his mother. Like Roger, he lost many family members to the famine.

"Could I go over to Emil's on Saturday?" Roger asked his mother one evening. "Emil says there are lots of old empty beer bottles in the ditches on the country roads. We're thinking we could gather a bunch in some sacks. He said his uncle will buy them off us."

With his mother's blessing, Roger was off with Emil on Saturday afternoon. The boys had a great afternoon returning with over fifty empty beer bottles.

At first, Maria was overjoyed with the new relationship since Roger was becoming much more positive. One day though, she overheard the two boys talking.

"I'd like to shoot all the damn Russians for what they did to my family," Roger exclaimed. "I hate them with a passion."

"Me too," Emil responded. "As my uncle always says, 'a good Russian is a dead Russian.'"

To her dismay, Maria realized that as the boys were growing older, their grief was turning to anger and hatred.

"I told my teacher a thing or two today," Roger spat out one evening as they were eating supper. "Today we were supposed to talk about our families. I told the class I only had my mom and my grandpa and that the rotten Russians had killed my baby sister and my tato. When I told the class how much I hated the Russians for what they did, the teacher said I should learn to forgive. I told him he didn't know what he was talking about because he never had any of his family murdered."

In Roger's thirteenth year, Emil moved to a town a hundred kilometres away and Roger was lonely again. In the years to come they visited occasionally, but mostly corresponded by letter.

The summer Roger turned fourteen; he and his mother were granted permission by the Russian government to return to Novich to visit their family's graves. The famine was long over and the Russian communist party had turned the small farms into larger collective ones. Maria and Roger stayed at Gregory's brother Roman's place on a collective farm a few kilometres out of Novich. Maria and Roger visited their old abandoned house and the graves. At times Roger's rage over the loss of his dad and sister came close to the boiling point, but he tried to keep control of his emotions. He knew it bothered his mom when he became enraged.

One day, Roger, with the help of his Uncle Roman, marked the graves with small crosses and erected a small picket fence around the burial site.

"You know, Uncle, Tato's and Elena's deaths make me so wild with the damned Russians," Roger said as they were finishing the fence. "Don't you hate the Russians for what they did to all of us?"

"Well, when I first heard of your tato's and Elena's deaths, I was both sad and angry, but you see, Roger, we've had our own pain. A month after you and your mom left, our twin daughters died of starvation. You must remember them. They were only nine months old."

"Yes I remember them. We visited you guys when they were born."

"That's right. You see there's no question that I hate what the Russians did, but I got over hating the actual soldiers, and I hope you will too. I found out that the anger and hate were causing me a lot of pain and getting me nowhere. Anyway, when I gave up on hating the Russian Army and those Ukrainians conscripted into the army, it helped me a lot. It helped me get on with my life. I finally realized that most of the people in the army were forced to do what they did or they would have been killed."

"I can't forgive those bastards," Roger shot back. "Never! Never! Never! I won't even try. If I did forgive those monsters it would be like saying that murdering my family was okay."

Roman shook his head and remained silent. Maria had told him of Roger's mind-set and he realized that arguing with him wouldn't do either of them any good.

Soon Roger and his mother were heading back to Poland.

On Sunday afternoon, Jacob picked Maria and Roger up at the train station.

"There are some changes coming into my life," Jacob announced, as they were driving back to the store. "I've been seeing Freda Schmidt. You'll remember her husband. He was that banker in Krackwich that died in that accident when his car was hit by the train."

"Yes I remember," Maria answered. "Wasn't that some eighteen months ago?"

"That's right. Anyway, we met at the club for widows and widowers that I've been attending for some time. Freda started attending a bit before you left for the Ukraine and of late we've been seeing each other."

"I'm happy for you, Dad," Maria replied in measured tones. "When can Roger and I meet her?"

"I've invited her for supper tonight. I hope that's okay with you. As old as I am, I must tell you I'm very attracted to her. I never thought romance would come my way again, but I guess it has. I've made a huge pot of borsch and Freda made a pie. I'll drop you and Roger off at the store and then pick her up."

"I hope she's a good woman," Maria commented to Roger as they were cleaning up the house. Maria mixed up a small batch of bread so they could have fresh bread with their borsch.

Maria and Roger were on edge when Jacob introduced Freda. She was an attractive, large lady with a Rubenesque figure. Although Maria thought that Freda talked a bit too much, the evening passed without incident.

At ten thirty, Jacob drove Freda home. Maria was still up when he got back.

"Well, what do you think of Freda?" Jacob asked expectantly. "She said she was impressed with you and Roger."

"She seems like a nice lady," Maria replied. "I was wondering if she's ever mentioned anything of her views on Jews, seeing she's German. From what I have gathered, the present German Government is quite anti-Jewish, but you no doubt can put my mind at ease on that matter."

"I can indeed. We've discussed the racial thing in depth and I can honestly say I can't discern the slightest bit of racial prejudice on her part. There was Jewish blood in her husband's family. Once you get to know her, I'm sure you'll find her a very open-minded lady. You probably noticed that like your mom, she's quite forthright. I admire that in a woman."

Over the next several months the relationship between Jacob and Freda became more serious and a marriage date was set. Maria and Freda were polite with each other and a degree of closeness was developing.

"Freda and I get along well," Maria commented to Roger one evening after Jacob and Freda had left. "I just wonder how things will work out for the four of us once she and Dad are married and we're all in the same house. It makes me feel so uneasy."

"I don't know. She's always pleasant with me too, but she kind of bosses Grandpa around and lets on she knows everything about everything. I guess that's what Grandpa wants though. It's kind of strange though that he'd be getting married after all these years. He must be getting close to seventy. I wonder how old she is. We get along, but she sure wouldn't be my pick for a wife. I wonder too about us living in the same house with them once they're married."

"I talked to Dad about that and he said Freda and he discussed it. According to him, Freda assured him that we would always be welcome to stay with them. They say that love is blind. I just hope and pray that Dad isn't being naive."

The Easter long weekend, Jacob and Freda were married in the synagogue in a neighbouring town. While the newlyweds went on a short honeymoon, Maria and Roger manned the store. Before the wedding, Freda moved much of her furniture and plants in. For want of room, Jacob moved his discarded furniture to his small vacant house at the end of the block.

The evening they returned from their honeymoon, Maria prepared a celebration supper and invited a few of Jacob's friends to join them.

"We should talk," Freda said as they were cleaning up after all the guests left. "I can't tell you how much Jacob and I appreciate this homecoming celebration. While we were away, Jacob and I were talking things over. No doubt in the future you'll be busy helping in the store so I'll cook. You could help me with some of the housekeeping if you'd care to."

"I think that will be okay," Maria replied, feeling in a no-win position. "We'll have to try hard not to get under each other's skin."

As time passed, Freda was starting to change. She was not above giving orders to everyone and she and Maria had a few disagreements. Finally, one evening, the two of them got into a heated argument.

"It's just not going to work out," Maria thought, as she lay in bed that night. "Freda feels she has to be in total charge of the household. It's not going to be possible for Roger and me to live here with Freda and Dad on a long term basis."

"I'm afraid it's going to cause a lot of problems for all of us if Roger and I stay with you and Freda any longer," Maria remarked to her dad the next morning when they were alone in the store.

"I'm so sorry. Freda promised me it would be alright, but I guess I was listening to my heart rather than my head. Without laying blame, I guess we should have known that it would be difficult for two ladies to live under the same roof. What would you suggest? I still want you and Roger to help me in the store."

"Well Roger and I can't live with you and Freda anymore or there will be a real blow-up. Both Roger and I feel our only option is to move out."

"What do we do? What do we do?" Jacob lamented. "Freda is my wife now, but you and Roger are my blood kin. Do you have any ideas?"

"You have that small vacant house at the end of the block. The house isn't that big, but it's sure big enough for Roger and me. There's all that old furniture of yours we moved there, so it's fully furnished. Roger and I would still like to work in the store, but this will give us all the breathing space we need."

"That sounds like a real good solution. Thanks for being so understanding."

Once Roger and Maria moved, relations between the two ladies became much more cordial again.

CHAPTER 4

Over the next few years, life was relatively good for Maria, Roger, Jacob and Freda. Although he still harboured hatred towards the Russians, Roger was doing well in school and proved a diligent worker in the store. Maria and Freda were becoming quite close. There were political rumblings of Germany again taking up arms though and that had them all concerned.

The much dreaded political upheaval and turmoil came to a head in 1939 when Germany invaded Poland. The Jewish community learned to their horror that the Nazis were making plans to implement their anti-Semitic program.

It wasn't long before SS soldiers were rounding up Jews for the slave labour camps or worse yet the extermination camps. Because they were of Jewish background, Jacob, Maria and Roger attempted to keep a low profile. Maria constantly prayed that they would be missed by the SS.

Maria worked in the store half time. Although Freda did not get involved with the running of the store, most days she had Roger and Maria stay for supper. Once Roger turned sixteen he quit school to work full time in the store. Like his dad, he had a swarthy complexion, was strikingly handsome and had a very husky build.

It was now fall and Roger had just turned 17. On a Friday, right after dinner, he and Jacob had gone out in the country to buy produce from farmers. Maria was left in charge of the store.

Jacob and Roger had been gone less than an hour when two SS officers walked into the store and approached Maria.

"We're looking for Maria Goodz," one of the officers began in broken Polish.

"That is me," Maria responded, her heart racing wildly.

"It says on this document that you are a Jew. Is that correct?"

Maria nodded, fear reflected in her eyes.

For some unknown reason, the officer showed Maria their list of names of people to be picked up. Although she saw her name, she noticed that neither Roger's nor her dad's names were on the list.

Realizing it was of great importance to try to save Roger and her dad, she added, "I was born in the Ukraine, but escaped here during the famine of 1933."

"Any relatives here?" the officer asked.

"Not here. A lot of them died in the famine. Those that are left, live in the Ukraine."

"You are being sent to a work camp. We will go with you to get a few of your work clothes."

Maria nodded. "I live down the street at the end of the block. Before I get my clothes, I should go upstairs and tell the store owner what's happening."

"We'll wait for you here, but be quick and don't try anything."

Maria rushed upstairs.

"There are two SS officers downstairs," Maria began, a look of horror in her eyes. "I was on their list of Jews to be picked up. "I glanced at their paper. Fortunately, Dad's and Roger's names aren't on the list. I told them I had no relatives here and that I came here to escape the famine."

Freda accompanied Maria back downstairs and accosted the two officers. "Have you gentlemen nothing better to do with your time than to take away our good workers?" she clipped in flawless German. "My brother is an officer in the German army and right now he's in the battle zone. Maria is such a good worker. Isn't there anything I can do to keep her here?"

"I'm sorry, Frau, but we have a job to do," the senior officer replied. "As you know, in the army, orders are orders."

"You go with the woman and get her clothes," the older officer said, turning to the younger one. "I'll catch up with you in a few minutes."

"This Maria says all her family are in the Ukraine," the officer continued once he and Freda were by themselves.

"Yes, that's what she's told me. She's a good worker, but doesn't share much of her private life."

"You said your brother is in the army. What is your name and how long have you lived in Poland?"

Freda recognized that she must not mention Jacob's name to the officers. Fortunately, she still retained her first husband's last name.

"I've lived in Poland for over thirty years," she continued. "My name is Freda Schmidt. I was born in Berlin. My folks lived there until their passing a few years back. My husband died a few years ago and I'm trying to keep the store going."

Satisfied that the apprehension and investigation of Maria was in order, the officer politely excused himself and caught up with Maria and the other officer.

When Jacob and Roger returned from the country in the late afternoon, there was no one in the store. They rushed upstairs.

"Do you have any idea where Maria is?" Jacob asked.

"It's not good news," Freda replied, visibly shaken. "Two SS officers came to the store about two hours ago. They said they were taking Maria to a work camp because she was Jewish. One soldier and Maria went to her house to get some clothes and then they drove off. Maria and I tried to protect you and Roger. Both of us told the SS officers that she came from the Ukraine during the famine and had no relatives in Poland. We're hoping that will protect the two of you, for the time being anyway. Here's a note from Maria for both of you."

With tears in his eyes, Jacob read aloud.

"I love you, Dad. I love you, Roger. Pray for me. We must try to keep strong and somehow stay in touch."

"It seems strange they would take Maria and not me or Roger," Jacob said shaking his head. "I warned Maria not to divulge to anyone that she was Jewish. I wonder if someone informed on her."

"The officer showed me their list for this village. Maria's name was on the list, but not yours or Roger's. The officer said they were in a hurry so they may not have talked to anyone else in the village. Who knows, I suppose there could have been an informer. Maybe Maria had a friend who might have unintentionally let the cat out of the bag."

Suddenly, a sick look came over Freda's face. "My brother William knows of my marriage to you, Jacob. I know he's very anti-Jewish. Years back he tried to persuade me not to marry my first husband because he was part Jew. That doesn't make any sense though. If he turned Maria in, why didn't he turn you in too?"

"First those Russian murderers and now the SS," Roger shouted. "Is there no justice in this world? Dad and Elena murdered and now Mom in a slave labour camp. There is no God. There can't be."

As the days slipped by, Jacob made a concerted effort to counsel his grandson, but Roger refused help. As in the past, he chose to turn his anger and hatred inward.

Roger still ate with Jacob and Freda, slept at his own place and continued to work in the store.

It was an early winter afternoon and approaching closing time. Jacob left Roger in charge of the store while he went to the post office at the end of the block to check on the mail. There was a letter from Claudia, a family friend who lived near the labour camp where Maria was interned. Claudia knew a friendly guard at the factory who occasionally gave her news on Maria. In the winter's growing darkness Jacob returned to the store. Roger was closing up for the day. He followed his granddad upstairs to the living quarters.

The twilight was deepening as Jacob opened the letter and then stood beside the window to read it. "God have mercy," he cried out in Yiddish. "It's a letter from Claudia. Maria died a week ago from pneumonia. My daughter, my daughter," Jacob sobbed. "We'll never see our Maria again. God help us all." With tears slipping down his cheeks, he collapsed at the kitchen table.

"Maria told me that her lungs have always been poor," Freda said, going over and placing a hand on Jacob's shoulder. "She probably caught a bad cold and no doubt pneumonia set in."

"It's those evil Nazis who are to blame," Roger snarled. "God, how I hate them and the Russians! They work people like they're animals and never enough to eat. Mama's gone," he said after a long pause, tears in his eyes. "First, there's Tato and my sister Elena to the Russians and now Mama." He stood in a daze. "There is no God," he spit out, his voice breaking. "If there was a God, he'd not let life be so cruel. How can we live with this? Why didn't the SS take me instead of Mama?"

"They probably would have if you and your grandpa had been on their list," Freda said. "All we can do now is hope and pray that somehow they'll miss you two. My friend in Krackwich says the SS have been making their rounds again."

"It's very strange the Nazis didn't know I'm Jewish," Jacob added. "Maybe they think I'm too old for the labour camps. After all, I'm seventy two."

"When they picked up Maria, they obviously didn't know about you and Roger. Somehow you two slipped through the cracks. Thank God both of you were out in the country that day."

"I can't believe it, my daughter is gone," Jacob moaned.

The following days were heavy as Jacob and Roger grieved the loss of mother and daughter. Freda did everything she could to comfort them.

A week after learning of Maria's death, they had just finished breakfast when two German soldiers and a translator came to the door. Fortunately for Freda, the officers were not the same ones who had taken Maria.

"You are Jacob Isaac," the translator said, turning to Jacob. "By this paper you're Jewish."

"That I am," Jacob replied, "but my wife was born in Germany. She is a Polish citizen."

"Yes our papers mentioned that. We're not looking for her. According to these records a Roger Goodz is employed in your store. It states here that he's your grandson."

"My grandson Roger works in the store and eats meals here." Jacob continued. "His dad and sister died in the Ukrainian famine of 1933."

The two officers had a brief conversation in German.

"You don't have to speak to us in Polish. We all speak German," Jacob interjected.

The officer nodded and continued in German. "You're half Jewish, right?" he said turning to Roger

Roger nodded, hardly able to breathe.

"There will be a truck here for the two of you in an hour. Have a few work clothes packed in a bag. You'll be going to a work camp about a hundred-fifty kilometres from here."

As the two officers turned to leave, the other soldier said in broken Polish. "Be here or this." With a sadistic grin, he drew his finger across his throat.

Freda helped Jacob put a few clothes into an old burlap sack. Roger went home, got his clothes and returned. In short order the soldiers were back to escort Jacob and Roger to the waiting truck.

"Try to send word on how you're doing," Freda whispered as she held Jacob's hand. "I'll never stop praying for both of you."

"Thank you my dear," Jacob replied, holding Freda close. "I'll love you forever. God be with us till we meet again."

CHAPTER 5

Roger and Jacob climbed into the back of a truck crowded with twenty or so men. They all sat bunched up on rough wooden benches.

Although it was early winter, the weather was quite mild. It was a crowded three hour trip to the camp. No one spoke. No one noticed the passing scenery. Everyone sat in a daze, apprehensive of what lay ahead. As they pulled into the work camp grounds, Roger saw scores of lean men working on huge piles of scrap metal. A Polish guard showed them to their barracks. Roger's and Jacob's hut was close to two hundred feet long with upper and lower bunk shelves on either side of a central hallway. Each sleeping compartment had a filthy straw tick for a mattress and a couple of dirty blankets. In front of their hut was a huge oak tree, close to thirty meters high and over a meter in diameter at the base.

Once the group had been assigned their sleeping spots, their Polish guard lined the men up in front of the barracks. In contrast to the slave workers, he was repugnantly fat. His expression was mean and his eyes cold.

"We are a recycling plant," he began. "You will be working from seven in the morning until seven at night, breaking, sorting and stock piling cast, steel, copper, aluminium and tin. Anyone not showing up for work or not working hard will be sent to our other camp. You know what we do with Jews there," he added with a macabre grin. "Anyone sent there doesn't come back. We eat at six-thirty in the morning and again at seven-thirty at night. Are there any questions?"

"Don't we get to eat at noon?" an older man next to Roger asked. There was deathly silence. The guard approached him and without replying, struck him hard across his face with his billy club. The old man sank to his knees, blood oozing from his nose.

"The next time you ask a question like that I'll send you to the other camp," the guard bellowed. "Do you understand?"

"I understand," the old man gasped, struggling to his feet.

"I would suggest that those of you who don't know German, learn it," the guard continued. "Some of the guards like me are Polish while some are German. Get on your work clothes if you've brought any and I'll take you to your work places."

Within minutes, Jacob and Roger had been placed in their work locations. Because he was robust and strong, Roger was assigned to the group breaking up scrap cast iron with sledge hammers. As Jacob, was becoming quite frail, he was placed in the group that sorted the different metals into piles.

"How did you make out?" Roger asked Jacob after they'd eaten supper and were walking back to their sleeping quarters.

"My work is tolerable. It's a little heavy for me, but I think I'll manage."

"I'll manage too," Roger growled. "Damn those Germans and the Polish who are helping them. I swear to God, if there is a God that someday I'll even accounts. They treat us like animals, feed us crap and then expect us to work like slaves. Screw them."

"A word of advice from an old man who has seen a lot of life. It's always best to try to swim with the current than against it if you're in a no-win situation. You'll save both physical and mental energy."

Roger shook his head and remained silent.

As the days slipped by, Jacob made a concerted effort to stoically accept his new lot in life with grace. Despite his grandfather's advice, Roger was inwardly, figuratively, frothing at the mouth with the injustices he observed. When they were together at the end of the day, Jacob was forever trying to get Roger to take a more objective view of their situation, but Roger was too full of anger and hatred to be rational. They worked their twelve hour shifts regardless of the weather. When it snowed or rained, the workers got soaked if they didn't have any rain gear.

Hartmann, a German guard, was a Godsend for Roger. He was in charge of Roger's group and had a kind disposition. Although the guards were not supposed to fraternize with the workers, Roger had the opportunity to tell Hartmann some of the pain he had in his life. Unfortunately for Jacob, Helmut, the guard in charge of his group was a cruel ogre.

A day didn't pass without one or more of the prisoners either dying or being removed. None of the workers knew what happened to the sick. No one dared ask. The cries and screams from the savage beatings never seemed to stop. At night one could hear the moans and groans of the workers, some sick, some suffering from injuries inflicted by the beatings, some slowly starving. The workers were trying desperately to hold on in the face of grim hopelessness. The rations were spare and the work hard. Often, there would be bodies lying outside their sleeping quarters waiting to be picked up; workers who had died in the night.

Roger became friends with Eli, a fifty-year old in his work group. Like Jacob, Eli had owned and operated a small store. Despite his age, he was in excellent physical condition and stronger than most men half his age. Eli was a Martial Arts Master and had taught martial arts prior to the war. Being older than most in his group, he became a father figure to a lot of the younger men.

"We're all in a no-win situation here," he told Roger one evening. "The only way we'll survive is to go with the flow rather than attempting to fight it. I've been watching you. You're a very angry young man. You've told me some of what you've gone though so I can appreciate where you're coming from. When I was young, I was angry too. My father saw this and got me into martial arts. It's helped me control my anger. Like you, I must fight that strong need to see justice done on a daily if not hourly basis. God only knows the urge I have to wipe out some of the cruel guards, but it's crazy to even think like that. We have to keep in line and try not to think of revenge. That's our one and only chance of surviving this hellhole."

The guards would not allow Eli to instruct in the martial arts, but after they had finished their day's work, he would show Roger and some of the other younger workers some defensive moves.

Hartmann was off for the day and Rubin, a despicably cruel guard, was filling in for him. Thomas, another close young friend of Roger's was in failing health because of T.B. and was not able to keep up with the group. Hartmann knew Thomas was sick and always saw to it that he had easier work to do. Not so Rubin.

"Get moving," Rubin bellowed running up to Thomas and hitting him hard across his back with the billy.

"But I can't," Thomas wheezed. "Please, I've got to catch my breath."

"You low-bred Jew! I'll teach you to slack off," Rubin screamed, laying a volley of blows to Thomas's back, shoulders and head.

Thomas collapsed. Had Rubin lain off, the matter may have ended there, but Rubin continued the beating. Suddenly, all hell broke loose. Both Roger and Eli rushed the guard.

"Get back, Roger," Eli barked; his eyes, wild with the killer glare.

Roger held back.

Rubin saw Eli coming and raised his billy club to ward him off. Rubin never saw what hit him. Eli was airborne, his dropkick knocking the guard on his back. With a deafening roar Eli caught Rubin with a vicious bone-breaking karate chop across the bridge of the nose just as he was getting to his knees. Eli whirled full circle for momentum and struck Rubin another vicious upward Karate chop under his nose, driving the fragmented bones up into his brain. The guard was dead before he hit the ground.

Roger could hardly believe what happened. Eli's attack was so sudden, so powerful, so vicious and so lightning quick. Eli looked up to see two other guards rushing to do battle, waving their billy clubs as they came.

Again Roger was amazed by Eli's skill, speed and strength. Using both his hands and feet, Eli had the guards lying unconscious in less than two minutes. Eli was standing, glancing down at the two prostrate guards when a shot rang out. Eli slumped to the ground.

A German soldier came running up, rifle in hand.

"That's one less Jew to worry about," he growled, flipping Eli over with his foot. Suddenly, Eli's hand flashed out, grabbing the rifle barrel. In a mini-second he was on his knees with the gun pointed at the soldier's chest. Another shot rang out and the soldier dropped.

As Eli sank down again, Roger was by his side.

"See what anger can do to you," he gasped. "Try to do as I said, not as I just did."

With his dying breath he whispered. "If you ever get out of this hellhole tell my wife what happened. Tell her I'll always love her."

There was one last sigh and then the life light slowly faded From Eli's eyes.

By now one of the guards had regained consciousness and was on his feet. He checked out Rubin, Eli and the soldier. Finding them all dead, he turned back to the workers.

"Back to work," he ordered. "We'll have the bodies removed shortly."

Thomas made a Herculean effort and slowly got to his feet. He fought to keep going for the rest of the day. Fortunately for him, the new guard was much kinder than Rubin. He witnessed Thomas being beaten and made allowances for him.

Hartmann was back doing guard duty the next day and as usual, saw to it that Thomas had the less arduous work to do.

Notwithstanding Hartmann's kindness, a week later, Thomas collapsed at work. Hartmann had Roger and a fellow worker carry him back to the sleeping quarters. Late that night with Roger sitting on the edge of his bed, Thomas passed away.

Both Eli's and Thomas's deaths weighed heavily on Roger. He half-heartedly tried to follow Eli's and Jacob's advice about not dwelling on the negative, but it was a losing battle. He dared not openly express his anger and hate, but as in the past, he turned his negative emotions inward.

Winter passed and it was now summer. Jacob tried hard to keep up at work, but slowly his health started to give out. He had congestion in his chest, a fever and was very weak. Years before he nearly died of pneumonia. Like his daughter, Jacob's lungs were not strong. One day Helmut hit him hard across the back for not moving fast enough.

"I don't know how much longer I can hold on," he said to Roger that evening as they were walking back to their sleeping quarters after eating. "I really don't know how I've kept going this long. I'm doing my best, but I know I have a high fever and my chest aches like it did in the past when I had pneumonia. Since Helmut hit me, my back isn't right. If anything happens to me, try to get word to your step-grandma if you can. You say that Hartmann is a kind man. If I don't make it, maybe he could get the message to Freda."

Jacob awoke the next morning, weak, delirious and so stiff he could hardly move his arms. He held on throughout the day on sheer willpower, but just a few minutes before quitting time he collapsed. Helmut came running up and began beating on him with his billy club.

"Get back to work you lazy Jew," he hollered as he flailed away on Jacob. "You'll quit when I tell you to quit."

Roger's group were on their way to supper, accompanied by Hartmann. As they were walking past the metal sorting compound they heard the altercation. Roger looked over to where the noise was coming from and realized to his horror that Helmut was beating his grandpa.

"You damned Nemsie," Roger screamed as he started running to his grandpa's aid. Hartmann tackled him. As Hartmann was helping Roger to his feet, Jacob had managed to get to his knees.

"Is this is how your superior Aryan race acts," Jacob cried out, "beating a defenceless old man who is too sick to work?" Blood was streaming from his nose.

Screaming out several oaths, Helmut hit Jacob two savage blows to his head.

Jacob collapsed.

"Roger, stay here while I talk to Helmut," Hartmann ordered. "The rest of you men, carry on to the kitchen."

A red-faced Helmut was standing over Jacob, club in hand. Hartmann squatted down and checked Jacob for vital signs.

"Nice going," Hartmann hissed with venom. "This is the second old man you've beaten to death in the last two weeks. We're at a work camp, not an extermination camp. Maybe you should transfer over to the death camp. You'd fit right in."

"Who the hell do you think you are, trying to throw your weight around?" Helmut growled. "You're sticking up for this damned Jew."

Hartman was a big man. He wrenched the club from Helmut's hand. Grabbing him by the lapels of his coat he lifted Helmut clear of the ground.

"If I hear one more peep out of you, you'll be looking at a Court Marshall," Hartmann roared. "Remember, I'm a lieutenant in the German army and you're not even a soldier. I'm doing guard patrol only because I was wounded in battle and volunteered to do so."

While they were talking, Roger came up to them, dropped to his knees and cradled his grandpa's head in his hands.

"Have the decency of leaving us alone now and go get someone to remove the body," Hartmann snapped at Helmut. "For your information, you've just killed this young man's grandfather."

With an angry scowl on his face, Helmut turned on his heel and strode off.

"My dido, my dido my dido," Roger wailed in agony, still holding Jacob's bloody head in his hands. "That useless animal has murdered my grandpa. He murdered him because he was old and sick. I'll even accounts!" he snarled, jumping to his feet and wiping his bloody hands on his pants. "I'll kill that bastard if it's the last thing I do."

"Come," Hartmann said, gently putting his hand on Roger's shoulder. "Let's go to the kitchen. Talk like that will either get you a one way ticket to the death camp or a bullet in the head. This war is hell. I guess I don't have to tell you that. I wouldn't mind ridding the earth of the likes of Helmut, but my hands are tied. This anti-Jewish bullshit is just that, pure bullshit. Still, I have to watch how far I push my agenda. It's a scary balancing act."

After a long pause, Hartmann continued. "You've told me of the loss of your Mother, Father and sister and now this. I can appreciate how you feel. Three months ago, just before I was wounded, I went home on leave. When I got to my home there was nothing left but a pile of rubble. The house had been destroyed by an enemy aircraft bomb." Tears slipped down his war-hardened face. "I lost my wife, my baby daughter and my invalid mother. As you know, the only reason I'm here is because I was wounded in action. I can assure you I'll be returning to action once I'm physically fit again."

"Yesterday, the camp's commandant told us guards that he got a call from a tank factory in Germany that needs fifty workers. I'm going to put your name in. I'm positive the conditions would be better there. What a pile of crap this Aryan stuff is. I can't say that enough times. Considering what's just happened, it's prudent for you to leave if you can. Helmut's nose is out of joint and without question he's small enough to be gunning for you if you stay on."

"Thanks. Anything would be better than this hellhole. Any idea when this would happen?"

"All of the guards are to meet with the commandant later this evening to give him our list of workers we recommend. Probably they will be moving the fifty men out tomorrow sometime. I know how full of hate you are towards Helmut for what he just did to your grandpa. You must promise me you won't try to do anything stupid towards him before you leave."

"It will be hard not to take him out, but as you said, that would be stupid. I promise. I'll get my revenge someday if we both survive the war."

Before they went for supper, Roger removed the small silver Star of David talisman from Jacob's pocket. After eating, Hartman accompanied Roger back to where Jacob had been murdered. The body had been removed, but there was still blood on the ground. In the growing darkness, Roger dug a small hole and placed the talisman in it. He then put a rock on top of the talisman and back-filled around the rock.

Roger slept very little that night as surges of anger and grief kept washing over him. He could see himself as a young boy, holding and playing with his grandpa's Star of David.

After breakfast, Hartmann approached Roger and a few of the other younger workers in his group and told them they had been chosen to go to the tank factory. Hartman instructed the other workers to pick up their clothes and be ready to leave.

When the others had left, Hartmann handed Roger a slip of paper. "This is my sister's address. Memorise it and then destroy it. I'd like to give you a word of advice. Try not to be consumed with hatred and anger over all the horrible things that have happened in your life. If you dwell on all the injustices and don't get rid of the venom, it will destroy you mentally. I know from first-hand experience. My dad is in a mental institute. He's a veteran of the First World War and couldn't or wouldn't rid himself of the anger and hatred he felt over the horrible war atrocities he witnessed. It finally got the better of him and we had to have him committed. The best of luck to you, Roger. Hopefully we can meet again after the war."

"I was wondering if somehow you could get word to my step-grandmother, Freda Schmidt and tell her of grandpa's death and me being shipped out. She's of German background and lives at my grandpa's store in Kozmin. Kozmin is close to the border with the Ukraine. Tell her I'll try to contact her after the war."

Roger hastily wrote out Freda's address and handed it to Hartmann. He then followed the others back to the barracks and got his clothes ready. Once Roger was by himself, he opened Hartmann's note and started to memorize the address.

He climbed into the back of a truck with a dozen other men and they left for the railway station. All the men broke into cheers as the despised labour camp faded from view. Soon they were aboard the train on their way to their new workplace in southern Germany. None of the men knew for certain what lay ahead, but all were hopeful that things would be better than they had been in the metal salvage work camp.

As the train pulled away from the station, Roger glanced back towards the infamous work camp. He was relieved that a horrible chapter in his life had come to an end.

CHAPTER 6

As the train moved out, Roger shut his eyes and tried to rest, but sleep would not come. Over and over again he could hear the groaning and screams from the old slave labour camp and then Helmut delivering the death blows to his grandpa. When the memories of the horrific work camp became too much to bear, he went back to repeating Hartmann's sister's address like a mantra.

Roger's group arrived late. After they were shown to their sleeping quarters, they were taken to the kitchen for a late supper. The factory complex was huge. The biggest part of the compound was the assembly plant where the tanks were being manufactured. A smaller section of the complex was the repair section. It was assigned for tanks retrieved from the battle zone that were in bad need of repair. Here they were disassembled and remanufactured.

At eight the next morning, the new recruits were given a tour of the factory and assigned to their job sites. Work would be from eight till six with a half hour off for lunch. Basically their jobs and working conditions were no different from those of the paid workers. The forced labourers were billeted on the factory grounds. Roger, like the majority of the recruits, was placed in the assembly section of the factory.

As Roger could speak German, his integration into the work force was less stressful for him than for the recruits who only knew Polish.

Roger had a mechanical inclination and was enjoying his work. After a week, he was fitting right in. Because of his good work ethic and ability, after a short time on the assembly line, he was assigned to the remanufacturing section of the plant. He worked with a group of twenty odd men disassembling the old tanks and itemizing the parts that needed to be replaced.

Without question, it was still a forced labour environment, but with each passing day Roger was feeling more comfortable about his new workplace. Not only did they have much better sleeping quarters, they were fed three meals a day. Though not fancy, the food was much better than at the other slave labour work camp. He recognized that the overall philosophy of this factory was productivity rather than punishment and experienced little discrimination from the paid workers. Roger's hard work soon began to show dividends.

Fritz, one of the foremen, was pleased with Roger's strong work ethic and mechanical aptitude. One day he asked Roger to stop in his office after work.

"I'm very impressed with your ability," Fritz began. "We need an extra hand to assist us in the rebuilding department. I've asked the supervisor if you could be moved here to help us out."

The next day Roger moved to Fritz's department and worked exclusively with him. Fritz was a short, husky, rotund, red-headed fellow with a kind disposition. Despite the factory's policy of regular workers not fraternizing with the forced labour group, a friendship developed between Roger and Fritz.

"You have a Ukrainian or Polish last name," Fritz said to Roger one day when they were taking a breather.

"Well my dad was Ukrainian and my mother Jewish. My mother and I escaped the famine in the Ukraine."

"So you must have gone through a lot then."

"It was hell." For the next few minutes, Roger detailed the horrible events that occurred in his past. "As they say, 'life's a bitch and then you die'. What about you? You have a Ukrainian or Polish name too. Did your family originally come from the Ukraine?"

"My dad left the Ukraine close to forty years ago. My mother is German. I learned a little Ukrainian from my dad, but not much. The way I see it, politics is all bullshit and all politicians are assholes. I know a little about the famine. Quite a number of my relatives in the Ukraine died because of it."

"You know, Roger, although you won't be allowed to apprentice as a mechanic, if you'd care to study some, I could bring you a bunch of the books on mechanics I used when I apprenticed. You say you can read some in German. I'm sure they'd help you. Maybe after the war, if you wanted to become a mechanic, you'd have a head start."

"Thanks for the offer. I'd love to go through the program. Even though it won't get me any points now, as you say, it could help me later on. Hopefully this stupid war can't last forever."

Roger had a fair amount of free time and was spending many hours immersed in the books Fritz supplied him with.

One afternoon, after being at the factory for many months, someone tapped Roger on the shoulder. He whirled around. There stood Hartmann.

"How are you making out?" Hartmann said as he shook Roger's hand. "I'm back in active service now. I'm on leave and thought I'd look you up. I've been talking to Fritz and he said you're doing very good work."

Fritz walked over and joined them.

"You guys need a place to talk," he said, escorting Hartman and Roger to his office. "Take as much time as you need."

"Well I managed to get in contact with your grandmother last week," Hartmann continued. "When we met she apologised for not being as mentally sharp as she used to be. She was very saddened, but not surprised by the news of Jacob's death. She was happy you had been moved here to the factory. I spent an hour or two with her."

"How is my grandma doing health-wise? How about the store? Is she running it or did she get someone to help her?"

"Other than having a bit of memory loss, she appeared to be okay physically. She told me she had no idea how to run the store so leased it to a couple and moved into the old house you and your mother lived in. That's where I met her. She was at wits end as what to do with the store. The people leasing it were not doing too well and had not been able to pay her the lease payments for several months."

"She said she was planning to hold out until Jacob or you returned, but with him dead and you being detained, if things didn't change, she'd be in a real bind. She said she hoped she wouldn't have to sell out and would only do so as a last resort."

"She spoke quite a bit about her memory getting bad. She mentioned that her mother suffered from dementia when she got older so her memory loss is becoming worrisome for her. She said that her brother is an SS officer stationed somewhere

here in Germany. She didn't have much good to say about him, though."

"We talked about you. We both hoped you could somehow rid yourself of the anger and hate you feel towards those responsible for your family's deaths. How are you doing in with those old memories?"

"Oh I guess I'm holding my own now. You'll remember I was pretty torn up while I was at the slave labour camp and especially after my grandpa's murder. It's better now as they treat us much better here."

"We'll have to try to stay in touch," Hartman concluded as they shook hands goodbye.

As the months slipped by, Roger continued doing well both at his job and at the mechanic courses he was studying in his spare time.

He had become good friends with Abe, one of his fellow workers. Abe, like Roger, had a Jewish mother.

"I have nothing but hatred for the Nazis," Abe said one day. "Last year my mother was taken away. We heard from a friend that she was sent to the gas chambers. The average German has no more love for the Nazi assholes than we have, but it's as much as anyone's life is worth to stand up and speak your mind."

Both Roger and Abe fed on each other's hate and anger. Both talked of people trying to get them to forgive. Both mocked the thought of forgiving.

Notwithstanding the advancements he was making and Hartmann's visit, Roger was still full of anger and hate over the loss of his family. He often fantasized on evening accounts with those who had caused him pain. His association with Abe wasn't helping his negative mental stance either. For the sake of survival, he was very careful to only reveal his inward feelings to a select few trusted friends.

Like Hartmann, Fritz was concerned with all the negative energy Roger harboured.

"Look, you've got to get rid of that hate and anger or it will start eating you up," he said one day after Roger had bared his inner anguish for the umpteenth time.

"It's easy for you to say that, but you haven't lost all your family to Stalin or Hitler."

"Maybe not, but you told me that Hartmann lost his family to the war and from what you said, he's getting on with his life."

"Hartmann is Hartmann and I am who I am," was Roger's cryptic reply.

Recognizing that any more discussion would be fruitless, Fritz shook his head and changed the subject.

It was now late in 1944. Roger had been at the tank factory for over eighteen months.

"How would you like to start writing your first and second year journeyman's exams?" Fritz asked Roger one day. "If one goes by the verbal tests I'm giving you, I'm sure you know as much of the theory of mechanics as I do. I know while the war is on it will be of no consequence, but if you were to write the exams, I would keep record of your marks. Once this war is over that would be of help to you."

"I'm game for it," Roger replied. "When and where can we do it?"

"Maybe we could start the first week in the New Year. You could write them in my office. No one needs to know what you're doing."

By the fifteenth of January, Roger had finished the exams and passed them with flying colours.

As winter dragged on, the war in the sky was being fought over Germany. The tank factory to date had escaped being bombed by the allies.

Early in the winter of 1945 rumours were rampant that the Allied forces had scored major victories and were poised to invade Germany. The workers were more concerned that the war would end rather than who would win it. Of late the rumour mill was heralding a certain German defeat.

The glorious day for Roger finally arrived. An executive of the factory, accompanied by an Allied officer called all the workers to the assembly hall.

"The war is over," the executive announced. "Germany has surrendered to the Allied forces."

It took a few moments for the news to sink in. Some of the workers cheered while others remained silent, disappointed that their country had been defeated. All were happy though, that there would be no more fighting.

"All of you that were in the forced labour section are free to leave," the officer said through the interrupter. "The factory will be closed until further notice."

"Thank God the damn war is over," Fritz said to Roger, once the officials had left. "Do you have any plans? I suppose you might want to go back home to see your grandma."

"Yes, I'd like to do that. You see when Hartmann stopped to visit me some time back he said that Grandma Freda had told him she was suffering from memory loss and was afraid of dementia. Harry, my older cousin is in the Polish underground army. Last month his wife, Anne, wrote me that Freda had been diagnosed with dementia and placed in a mental home. At any rate, now that the war is over I'm hoping it won't be too hard for me to get into Poland to visit her."

"Well, if you have no immediate plans, you're welcome to stay at my place for the time being. My home isn't all that big, but you're welcome to stay with us until you find a place. I live in Demzig. My brother Claus and I own a small garage there. I'm sure we'd have work for you in the garage."

"You don't know how much your offer means to me. After being under the thumb of the Nazis for so long, it feels good to be able to make decisions for myself again. If it doesn't put your family out too much, I'd be happy to take you up on that offer."

By early afternoon Roger and Fritz were on the road. Gretel, Fritz's wife, was at the door to welcome them. She, like her husband, was not a great Hitler fan and was overjoyed that the war was over. That night they all drank a little too much as they celebrated the war's end.

The next day Gretel helped Roger with the paper work to allow him to go to Poland to visit his grandma for compassionate reasons. They knew that Poland was now under Russian control and were told by the government agent that it might take a long time to get all the paper work processed.

Gretel and Fritz were great hosts, but Roger wanted his independence. Within a week, he found a room of his own, half a block from the garage. Claus, like Fritz, was also outgoing and kind. Roger was fitting right in and they soon had him officially on the apprentice program.

After several months of waiting, Roger's visiting visa came through and he was on the train for the long train ride back to Eastern Poland. The trip was made longer as some of the rail-lines had been bombed out, making for lengthy detours. Roger would be staying with his cousin Harry on their small farm a few kilometres from the home where Freda lived. With the war over, Harry had just returned from the Polish underground army.

Harry and his wife picked Roger up at the railway station. It had been many years since the cousins had seen each other.

"So good to see you again," Harry began, shaking Roger's hand. "We're happy you survived that horrible work camp. We sure have a lot of catching up to do."

"Welcome back," Anne said, giving Roger a hug. "I'm afraid the news on your grandma is not all that good. With Harry serving in the underground army, I tried to keep in contact with her ever since you and your grandpa were taken away. Sometime after you and your grandpa left, her memory started to go, but she was still managing. After spending some time in the hospital though, she didn't seem the same. Whether it was the all the stress of your mom, you and Jacob being sent to slave labour camps or just old age, over time her mind really started to slip. Finally, a few months before the end of the war her brother, William, had her put into a long-term care home. She doesn't recognize us most of the time. Maybe the three of us could go see her tomorrow."

"We can swing by Kozmin and look at the old store and your old house," Harry added. "The store was abandoned for some time and just recently reopened. As you know, we're under Russian occupation now so nobody seems to know anything or if they do they're afraid to talk. Who knows if living under Russian rule will be better than living under the Nazis? In my opinion all governments are corrupt. Pardon me for being cynical, but I've seen so much horror while being in the underground army. I'm thinking that for the most part, life is all bullshit."

"After what I've gone through with all my family killed either by the Russians or the Nazis, I couldn't agree more," Roger replied. "Do you have any idea what happened to Grandpa's other property and his money? I know he used to have quite a bit of property and investments."

"I think we both have to be very fearful for Grandpa's estate. From what the hospital told us; William, Freda's brother, put himself in charge of Freda's affairs before she was hospitalized. William now lives in West Germany. The matron said he claimed to be Freda's next of kin. This was while Poland was still under German control. I guess you and I are the only ones of Jacob's line that are left. I've tried to contact William, but so far I've had no luck. The hospital tells me he still has the power of attorney over all her affairs. I imagine he must hold all of Jacob's and Freda's assets in trust and will do so as long as Freda is alive. After she passes on, what will happen with Jacob's estate is anyone's guess. Damn those Nazis anyway. With Germany losing the war, who knows?"

"If you find out anything that's happening here, you could contact me," Roger added. "If I find out anything when I'm back in Germany, I'll let you know."

"I think that's a plan. When we visit Freda, we should talk to the hospital matron and try to get the facts straight about who's in charge of what."

Roger, Harry and Anne spent the evening getting caught up on their lives. In the morning they were on their way to visit Freda. When they arrived at the home, they stopped at the matron's office.

"I'm sorry folks, but as you will see, Freda has slipped quite a bit since your last visit," the matron said. "Although she eats well with some assistance and her physical health seems fair, of late, her mind has really deteriorated. She doesn't recognize or acknowledge any of the staff anymore."

"I'd like you to meet my cousin, Roger," Harry responded. "His father and sister died in the Great Ukrainian Famine. Roger and his mother, Maria, escaped the famine and lived with Jacob. Shortly after Jacob married Freda, he, Maria and Roger were all sent to slave labour camps. Only Roger survived."

"Pleased to meet you," the matron said shaking Roger's hand. "My heart goes out to you for the loss of your family."

"Thank you," Roger replied. "War is hell."

"It's sad that our grandma's mind has deteriorated so much," Roger continued. "We were wondering if you have any idea of what's happening with our grandfather's business interests."

"Freda's brother, William was made her trustee when she was incapable of making decisions on her own. He brought her here to the home when she couldn't look after herself. William told me he had taken on power of attorney over her affairs."

"Yes, we're aware of that," Anne replied. "While she was still in control of her faculties, Freda told me that Jacob had left everything to her and at her death, Jacob's estate was to go to Roger and Harry as they were his only remaining heirs. She said when they married it was agreed that her estate would go to her family and Jacob's estate to his family. Our hands were tied as Harry was half Jew. He was in the underground army and Roger was in a slave labour camp. As William was a high ranking officer no one dared interfere. Of course by that time Freda was mentally pretty well out of it."

"A lot of shady dealings happened in the war," the matron continued. "I'm afraid I have no more knowledge regarding Freda's brother and the estate. I've tried several times over the last two years to get a hold of William to tell him how his sister was doing, but with the war going on, I've had no luck. The home address he gave me is in Allied-occupied West Germany. With the war just over, it's going to take some time to get things sorted out and back to normal. We're now under Russian control, of course, so there are mountains of red tape for everything."

Roger's, Harry's and Anne's visit with Freda was a total disappointment. Although she seemed in reasonably good physical shape, there wasn't the slightest flicker of recognition on her face when they met. After staying with her for close to an hour, they left.

When they stopped at Jacob's old store, they found it open. At the small village inn they learned that before the end of the war the funeral home director was also acting as a real estate agent. Before leaving Kozmin, they dropped in at the funeral home.

"You'll have to understand that since the government changed I no longer handle real estate," the funeral director said. "While I was still handling real estate, I was approached by a German officer. He showed me papers that substantiated that he was Freda Schmidt's brother and had power of attorney over her affairs because of her mental condition. He told me that Freda's husband, Jacob, had died and said that in Jacob's will all his estate was left to Freda. He had me list all of Mr Isaac's properties. The two houses and the store were sold and as he requested, I sent the funds to him. Shortly after the store was sold, the war ended. The Government of course is new and knows nothing so to get any information from them is like pulling hens' teeth. I have no idea what happened with Jacob's other finances. You'll have to try contacting William. At the time I was doing business with the lieutenant I got the gut feeling that some skulduggery was going on, but for my own welfare I wasn't about to question a high ranking Nazi officer."

Feeling they had accomplished little, Roger, Harry and Anne returned home.

For Harry and Roger, it was an evening of regurgitating the injustices of life, the horrors of the war and the famine. Over a bottle of vodka they fed on each other's anger and hate. Anne couldn't abide them flailing around in their respective pools of self-pity, so went to bed early.

The next day dawned sunny and warm. As it was Sunday, Anne made a picnic lunch and they spent the afternoon at a small lake. Both gentlemen were hung-over and tired so conversation varied from light to non-existent.

On Monday, Harry drove Roger back to Kozmin to see if he could find the whereabouts of his old childhood friend Emil and his family. From Emil's uncle, Roger learned to his horror that Emil and his family had all been sent to the gas chambers.

"Life's all a rotten joke," Roger growled to Harry as they drove back to the farm. "Emil was a good friend, but oh no, God says, 'Roger doesn't need a friend.' Those slimy Nazis. God's no better than the Nazis or Russians for letting all this killing happen."

"Yeah, life's a total bitch," Harry responded, shaking his head.

"I was feeling pretty down after seeing Freda and learning that Jacob's estate has been stolen by William," Roger said to Anne once they got home. "Now I find out God has another treat for me. I just found out my best friend and his family were executed by the Nazis. Doesn't life suck?"

Roger would be catching the train in the morning. In the time they had left with him, Harry and Anne did their best to bring him out of his funk, but all to no avail. Roger headed back to Germany a very depressed young man. If anything, his visit only amplified his anger and hate.

CHAPTER 7

The next several months were heavy for Roger. Time did lessen the pain though and with Fritz and Claus spending many hours talking to him, he was slowly getting control over his depression.

Work was going well. Roger challenged and successfully wrote his journeyman mechanics exams. After being with Fritz and Claus for the better part of two years, Roger suffered a work-related accident. He broke a bone in his foot when an engine block fell on it. His foot was put in a cast and he was hospitalized for some time. Once the cast was removed, the doctor stopped in to see Roger.

"We're going to try to get you back walking as soon as possible. It may hurt a bit, but we've pinned the broken bone so the sooner you can start moving about, the better. You know how much pain you can abide so you'll have to be your own governor. Later this afternoon we'll have Corrine, a nurse's aid, give you a hand to help you get moving."

After dinner, Roger was given some pain killers. Soon he fell asleep.

"Roger, Roger, wake up."

Someone was gently shaking his shoulder.

"I'm sorry, I must have dropped off," Roger responded glancing upward.

Roger was looking into the most beautiful face he'd ever seen. When their eyes met it was like a current of electricity was arcing between them. There was an immediate, strong, physical attraction for both of them.

Corrine was fairly tall, blonde, blue eyed, buxom and had striking Nordic features. She was from Northern Germany and began working in the hospital as a practical nurse a few months after the war ended.

"The doctor is right about it being painful," Roger groaned as Corrine assisted him in his first few steps. "I guess we'd better keep at it though."

Despite the discomfort in his foot, Roger felt quite titillated as he shuffled along, holding on to this beautiful girl for support. On Roger's insistence, they walked more than they should have. From what Roger gathered, Corrine was unattached.

"I was wondering maybe if you'd care to visit me some evening," Roger said as Corrine was taking him back to his room. "It gets pretty lonely here and the doctor says I'll be here for several more days."

"That would be nice," Corrine replied, blushing. "I get lonely too. All my family and close friends are back in Northern Germany. My dad died a few years ago. My mother remarried, but I don't get along too well with my step-father. That's the main reason I moved here. I'll drop by this evening."

Roger had just finished eating supper when Corrine stopped in. After making light conversation for a few minutes, Corrine turned the focus on Roger.

"What about your background? You speak fluent German, but you don't have a German name and I noticed you have a bit of an accent."

"Well you see, my dad was Ukrainian and my mother Jewish. As to my background, it's pretty heavy stuff."

"If talking about it would bother you, you sure don't have to."

"No that's alright. I should tell you a bit about my past. You see I was nine years old when the famine came to the Ukraine. It's almost too horrible to imagine. I have so much hatred for those damned Russians who starved us. I will never forget that haunting sound of my little sister crying for food. When she grew too weak to cry anymore she just whimpered. The night she died my mother was rocking her in her arms chanting over and over again 'Hospodeh Pohmiloy'('God have mercy'). I remember Elena's breathing getting shallower and slower. I wanted desperately to somehow speed it up. Dad and I were sitting by Mom, crying. The whimpering grew weaker and then stopped. For a moment a faint smile crossed her little face and then she died in Mama's arms." Roger could not go on. He fought for control, but tears were soon slipping down his cheeks.

"I can't imagine the pain you're bearing," Corrine whispered, coming over to Roger and holding him close. "There's so much pain and cruelty in this world, so much. What about the rest of your family?"

It took Roger some time before he blurted out, "I don't really have anyone else. Those Russian dogs executed my dad just after my sister died. All of us were starving and his crime was stealing a small bag of wheat to feed us. The Nazis were no better. Mama and I escaped to Poland to my grandfather's place. Because my mama was Jewish, she was taken to a slave labour camp and died there. Later my grandfather Jacob and

I were taken to another slave labour camp. I watched a guard beat my grandfather to death."

"I can't talk about it anymore," Roger added, fighting for control. "I'm trying to put it out of my mind. If I think on it too much I get so mad I can't sleep."

"I'm so sorry, Roger. If I had known the pain it would cause you, I'd have never asked. It hurts me so much to see the anguish in your eyes."

"That's okay," Roger responded after pulling himself together. "I really shouldn't be burdening you with my old nightmares. You see my early childhood was very happy. Then the famine came and after that the war. Instead of going on about me, tell me about your life."

"Well, I come from a small village in Bhremerland. That's on the northern coast of Germany. I had a good childhood. I was especially close to my dad. He was so easy-going and never got into a dither over anything. Dad was much older than Mom. Three years ago he died. I miss him so much. Anyway, a year later, Mom remarried. Why she married Fredric, I'll never know. He was quite a few years younger than Mom. He is very controlling and a staunch believer in all this Aryan superiority bunk. I tried to get along with him, but I couldn't stand his diatribes against the Jews so I left home. I took a nurse's aid course and after graduating, I headed south. I started working here after the war ended."

"I start working at seven in the morning so I should be going now. I'll see you again in the afternoon." Corrine went over to Roger and gave him another hug.

"I'll sure be looking forward to that," Roger whispered, holding Corrine close for a long moment.

Corrine continued to assist Roger with his rehabilitation for the rest of his stay in hospital and always dropped by in the evenings after work for a visit. A week after his rehabilitation began, Roger was discharged. Before he left the hospital he phoned Gretel and asked her if he could bring Corrine over later in the evening.

Roger was waiting for Corrine when she got off shift and they went out for supper.

"I invited us over to Fritz's and Gretel's place this evening for coffee," Roger said as they were eating. "I hope you don't mind. I'd kind of like to show you off. They're very big-hearted people."

"I look forward to meeting them. You've told me a lot about them. We won't be able to stay out too late. I have to work tomorrow and I need my sleep if I'm going to be working the next day."

"So this is the young lady who taught you to walk again," Fritz quipped when he met Corrine. "I can see now why you said getting back on your feet was painfully enjoyable, Roger."

Corrine and Roger spent a very relaxed evening with Fritz and Gretel, but left early.

The next afternoon Roger was waiting for Corrine when she got off work.

"I've been thinking all day about your horrible memories from the past," Corrine said as they walked to Roger's apartment. "I was wondering if you ever tried meditating."

"No, I'm not into that kind of thing."

"Well I've been doing meditation for the last year or so and it seems to keep me balanced. The other night though, I had a very strange vision while I was meditating. It was pretty scary. If you're up to it, I wouldn't mind sharing it with you."

"Go for it. I remember my mama was into that stuff. She used to talk about it to my grandpa and me. She figured that maybe meditating would help me with the memories of Elena and Dad dying, but as I just said, that isn't my sort of thing. Go ahead."

"Okay, it helps if I can share these visions with someone. Ever since I was young I've had this strange thing about myself. It's kind of scary, but the odd time I can see into the future. It's hard to understand, but I knew quite some time ahead of his death that my granddad would die in a farm accident. In this vision I saw him being crushed by a farm tractor. I was about ten at the time. When I told this to Mom, she laughed. 'Your grandpa is as healthy as a horse. He's only in his fifties. You've been daydreaming too much.' Almost to the day, a year later, the tractor he was driving rolled, instantly killing him. With my dad's death, I had this vision that he would die in a month of a heart attack while out for a walk. He was in fairly good health at the time. Anyway, a month later, he and Mom were out walking and you guessed it, he dropped dead of a heart attack."

"Now, this vision I had the other night is hard to figure out. It involved you, but you looked like you were middle-aged. At any rate, the frightening part was that you seemed to be agitated. You had blood on your face and were in a strait jacket. The picture flashed across my mind's eye and was gone."

"You're a wonder," Roger replied, chuckling. He reached over and took Corrine's hand. "When you look into your crystal ball do you see anything pleasant about us being together in the future?"

"That is a pleasant thought, but strangely, I never see the things that involve me, only the things involving those close to me."

"Of late, I can't get over how much my thinking is changing," Roger said to Corrine later that evening as they were walking hand in hand by the river. "Ever since you've come into my life, my past is haunting me less."

"It's kind of that way with me too. I used to be upset at the universe for the pain in my life and it sounds like it was the same for you. Since I've met you, life looks so much brighter."

"I spend every minute of the day looking forward to being with you in the evenings," Roger added. "It's strange. A few years back I honestly didn't think I'd survive long enough to see the end of the war, and now here we are with so much to look forward to in the future."

"I'll bet you can't guess what my worst fear was when I was in that first slave labour camp," Roger said later when they got back to Corrine's place.

"The way your hands seem to wander when we're close, I'd have to say it has to have something to do with the opposite sex. I suspect that's the male thing," she quipped pushing Roger's hand away.

"Yeah, sort of I guess. You see I had a crush on a girl just before I was taken to the slave labour camp, but nothing ever came of it. I remember feeling so lonely. Seeing men dying around me in the camp I was terrified that I would die without, you know ever . . . ."

"Let me guess. Was it something about finding a girl you loved and who loved you and being intimate with her?"

"You must be able to read my mind," Roger replied, smiling. He pushed Corrine down on the couch, half lay on top of her and they were soon into some heavy necking.

Roger unbuttoned Corrine's blouse, unhooked her bra and began playing with her breasts. As his hand slipped under the waist band of her skirt she blurted out, "We have to stop. We agreed we wouldn't go all the way and besides it's the dangerous time of the month for me. It's only been a month since we met, you know. I love you dearly, but don't you think we're rushing things a bit?"

"Although I'd love to go all the way with you, I guess I promised."

"I don't know," Corrine replied, running her hand seductively over Roger's bare chest. "I know it's hard for you to be patient. We've talked about getting married. Maybe after we get engaged we can be intimate."

As Roger disentangled himself from Corrine a cloud came over his face.

"I'll never forget Thomas. He was about my age and worked with my group breaking up cast iron in the slave labour camp. We often talked about the day we'd be free. Like me, he longed for a girlfriend and we talked of someday having our own families. Poor Thomas got T.B. Maybe he had it before he came. I don't know. Those cruel Nazis showed him no kindness. They forced him to keep working. I was sitting on his bunk beside him the night he died. 'If you can, try to tell my mother what happen,' he gasped. 'I hope you survive this hell hole and someday find a girl to love.' Those were his dying words."

"I managed to get back to Poland a few months back and tried to look up my old school chum Emil. I discovered that he and all his family died in the gas chambers. Damn those evil Nazis anyway," he growled. "I hope they all rot in hell. I'd better smarten up and think of something else or I won't be able to sleep tonight."

Although Roger fought hard to control his emotions, he broke down. Corrine held him until he regained his composure.

CHAPTER 8

Three months into their relationship, Roger bought Corrine her engagement ring. That evening they went for a walk by the river. In the growing darkness, Roger slipped the ring on her finger.

"I love you so much!" Corrine exclaimed. "I'll love you forever."

"I'll love you forever too. Now what about that 'being intimate thing.' A while back you mentioned something like 'we'd have to wait until after we were engaged'."

"Why not," Corrine replied seductively. "You're a sly one. I see you came prepared. I wondered why you brought a blanket with you."

It had been a beautiful warm day. They found themselves a secluded grassy spot, adjacent to the trail. There, they spread the blanket. After making passionate love they lay in each other's arms savouring their new closeness.

"That was just so beautiful," Corrine whispered. "Now don't you think it was worth waiting for?"

"It sure was," Roger sighed. "After we get back to your apartment, maybe we should try again."

The minute they got back to Corrine's apartment, she was on the phone to her mom, Helga and her younger sister, Rena.

"I have wonderful news," she blurted out. "Roger just gave me my engagement ring. I've never been so happy in all my life. We're planning on getting married in about four months."

"I'm happy for you," Helga replied. "From what you've told us, Roger must be a wonderful guy."

"You're a lucky girl," Rena cut in. "You can be sure that Mom and I will be there for the wedding."

"Your step-dad is away quite a bit with his work," Helga continued. "If he can't drive us down, Rena and I will come by train."

Corrine and Roger stayed up late making wedding plans.

"It's sad, but there won't be many guests on my side," Roger said. "All my family are gone except Grandma Freda, Cousin Harry and his wife. Freda's mind hasn't improved so she's out of the question. As for any of my kinfolk left in the Ukraine, they will be in the Russian-occupied territory so they won't be able to make it."

"Let's just have a small wedding then," Corrine suggested. "You won't have any family coming and I'll only have Mom and Rena."

"That's okay by me. Really, we can only afford a small wedding. Maybe we should just have your mom, sister and a few of our close friends. It sounds like your step-dad probably won't make it. I'll try to get a hold of Hartmann. The last time I saw him was before the end of the war at the tank factory. I'd sure like him to attend. I still have his sister's phone number. I'll contact her and see if she knows his whereabouts."

The next few weeks flew by for Corrine and Roger. They were very much in love and relishing their new found closeness. Both of them were happy that the memories from the past were growing fainter for Roger.

A week before the wedding, Helga and Rena arrived at the train station. Roger and Corrine picked them up.

"I've heard so many positive things about you," Helga said when she met Roger. "I'm so glad my Corrine has found a good man. I certainly had one with her dad."

"Thank you," Roger replied. "I'm happy that Corrine has your support. She's a wonderful girl. It's uncanny how you, Corrine and Rena look so much alike."

"Yes, I guess there is a strong resemblance," Helga continued. "When Corrine was still at home, the three of us entered a mother daughter look-alike contest and we won first prize."

With the wedding fast approaching, the ladies were hard at it with all the preparations. Roger gave a hand once he got home from work.

A few days before the wedding, Roger phoned Hartmann's sister. She advised him that Hartmann had remarried and gave Roger his phone number.

"My name is Roger Goodz," Roger said when he got through to Elsie, Hartmann's wife. "Hartmann and I are old friends from the war years."

"Yes, I recognize the name. Hartmann has talked of you. Unfortunately he's not here right now. He had back surgery a week ago and now is in a rehab centre. I'll be seeing him tonight. I know he'll be glad you called. I'll give you a phone number at the rehab centre so you can talk to him yourself."

"I looked on Hartmann as sort of my surrogate father," Roger said to Corrine that evening. "He's helped me so much."

"You know where he is now so why don't you drive over and look him up tomorrow? You're on holidays now and everything is pretty well ready for the wedding. It's only a three-hour drive. You'll just have to remember to be back by eight for the rehearsal."

Roger phoned Hartmann and by six the following morning he was on the road. Roger was taken aback when they met. Hartmann was slowly shuffling along the hall with the assistance of a walker. Roger followed him back to his room.

"Sit," Hartmann said, pointing Roger to a chair. "I'm so glad you contacted Elsie. We've got a lot of catching up to do. The war was still going full bore when we last visited at the tank factory."

Hartmann slowly sat down across from Roger, pain etched on his face.

"As you probably learned from Elsie or my sister, I was wounded again in action just before the end of the war."

"Yes, they both mentioned that."

"I thought I had it made," Hartmann said with a smile. "I had of course returned to duty when I visited you in the tank factory. Because of my old injury, I was helping in a support roll. Then a few months later, as the Allies started putting the pressure on us, we began fighting in a rear guard action and I was again in the thick of it. A month before the end of the war I got hit in the back by shrapnel. The doctors didn't think I'd ever walk again, but as you see, I manage to shuffle along with a walker. With this surgery the doctors are hoping I'll be able to manage better, possibly without the walker or a cane. So that's my story. What about yours?"

"Well, when we last visited at the tank factory, things were going good for me. I got along real well with Fritz, our foreman. After the war I started to apprentice in his and his brother's garage and I got my journeyman's papers. A few months ago I met Corrine, a nurse's aid and we're getting married on Saturday. Corrine and I would like you and your wife to attend, but I can tell you're in a lot of pain. It's good to see that you're still hanging in there. Doesn't it make you sort of pissed off with life though?"

"I'm glad to hear you're getting on with your life. As to being wild about what happened to me, we talked about that before and how anger and hatred were my dad's downfall. Dad is still totally immersed in his anger and hatred. I've about given up on him. He's in his late eighties and still hospitalized. He seldom talks, but when he does it's the same old crap. He continues to wallow in his self-made pool of pity about all the injustices of the universe. If anything, his bitterness is getting worse."

"As for me, I'm managing quite well. Now, what about you? I recall you were still having a few problems with your anger and hate when we last talked at the tank factory."

"It's a lot better now with the war over. It's still in the back of my mind, but now that I've met Corrine, I'm thinking of it less and less."

"That's good. You talked to Elsie. We married four months ago. She was an old classmate. She's a high school teacher. Her husband was in the army and died in the war. Our marriage has been very healing for both of us. I'm an accountant. It was sort of slim pickings right after the war, but now things have started to pick up."

"Do you remember Helmut?"

"How could I ever forget a devil like him? There were lots of other guards that were devils, but he was the worst.

If I ever get a chance I'll even accounts with that monster for murdering Grandpa."

"You won't have to worry about doing that now. He met a horrible death about a week before I went back to active service. As you'll recall, I took him to task for the senseless murder of your grandfather. From there on out he gave me a wide berth. I think he realized I was gunning for him. Anyway, you remember them shunting the scrap metal cars around when they were moving them out?"

Roger nodded.

"Well, they were moving the train back to couple up a car. Somehow, Helmut either slipped or was pushed between the hitches of the two cars. The hitches went right through his chest. I guess that old saying, 'what goes around comes around' has some truth to it."

"I can't say I'm going to shed too many tears over that news," Roger interjected acidly. "The rotten bastard got what he deserved."

Roger and Hartmann spent several enjoyable hours together. Again and again, Hartmann stressed the necessity of Roger ridding himself of the negative and embracing the positive.

"It's been so nice to see you again," Hartmann said as they shook hands goodbye. "I'd love to attend your wedding, but with my back the way it is that won't be possible. The best of luck to you and Corrine. You've come a long way in not letting your anger and hatred from the past rule your life. Keep up the good work. We'll have to stay in touch."

As Roger was driving back to Demzig, he was preoccupied with all the rough breaks Hartmann had in his life. "First losing his family to the war and then ending up with a broken back," he muttered. "Damn the universe anyway. Why does crap always happen to the good guys?"

When Roger arrived back from visiting Hartmann, he was just in time for the rehearsal. After the rehearsal, Corrine made him a late supper.

"Hartmann's case makes you wonder about the fairness in life," Roger said after finishing supper. "Just imagine coming home to your family and finding nothing but a heap of rubble where your house used to be. Think of the pain of finding out your wife, daughter and mother had been killed in a bomb blast. Like me, he lost most of his family to the war and to top it all off, now he's a cripple. Hartmann's a real good sort, but I don't know. He's forever trying to feed me this line on forgiving and forgetting the terrible things that happened in my life. Maybe Hartmann can do that, but not me. No way. To me that would be like saying the murder of my family was okay. No damn way."

"Each of us handles our emotional pain differently," Helga interjected. "Any method we use is okay, I think, just as long as we control our pain and the pain doesn't start controlling us."

"Yes, you're right," Roger replied. "I know for the sake of Corrine and myself, I've got to keep control of my memories and not let them overpower me."

Later that evening, after Roger left, Helga contacted Fredric, her husband, by phone.

"The wedding is on Saturday and I just wanted to make sure you were coming down. The wedding is at two o'clock. If you got an early start, you'd be here in plenty of time. Rena and I could go back with you after the wedding rather than taking the train."

"In all honesty, I don't think I can attend," Fredric replied hesitantly. "I guess I should have mentioned this to you before you left, but I didn't want to cause a hassle. I certainly wish Corrine well, but I don't approve of her marrying anyone of Jewish background."

"You idiot," Helga hissed. "Did you not learn anything from the war? You're still a bone-headed racist Nazi! Let me assure you that you'll be pulling up your socks when we get back or that's it for our marriage." Before Fredric could reply, Helga hung up.

"I think for now, Mom, it would be wisest not to mention the phone call to Roger," Corrine stated. "He's suffered so much painful discrimination. I'm not sure how he'd handle it. As for Fredric, I see the creep hasn't changed any. He's still as much the narrow-minded bigot that he was when I left."

"I'm so ashamed. As I just told that rectum, I can guarantee there's going to be real changes when I get home or he'll be looking for a new place to stay. It's my house we're living in. I've had about enough of his repugnant attitude."

Saturday, at two, a very nervous bride-to-be, accompanied by her mother, walked down the aisle to an equally nervous groom. Rena was Corrine's maid-of-honour while Fritz stood up for Roger. Once Pastor Burkholder had finished with the exchange of vows, he had the newlyweds sit in a small pew to the side of the pulpit for his address. Roger and Corrine could see both the minister and the guests. Burkholder just began his sermon when Corrine noticed something quite odd. There were two people standing at the back of the church, a dark complexioned man who looked in his mid-thirties and a fine-featured blonde lady, perhaps in her late twenties, holding a beautiful little blond girl. Corrine nudged Roger. She was just going to ask him if he knew who the three were when to her amazement, they disappeared.

"Did you notice those people standing at the back of the church when Pastor Burkholder started his sermon?" Corrine asked Roger as they were going to get the wedding pictures taken. "I thought they might be your relatives as the man so closely resembled you. Come to think of it, I've never seen a picture of your folks. Anyway, I was going to ask you who they were and when I glanced back at them again, they were gone."

"I didn't notice anyone. I have no idea who they could have been. Maybe they came to the wrong wedding, who knows."

After the reception, Roger and Corrine returned to Roger's apartment. They would leave on their honeymoon in the morning. Helga, Rena, Fritz and Gretel plus a few of Corrine's and Roger's friends dropped over and soon the wine was flowing freely. Corrine was still perplexed with whom the three visitors at the back of the church were. Like Roger, none of the other guests had seen them either.

"There's something so odd about their sudden appearance and disappearance," Corrine said to Roger. "I don't suppose you'd have a picture of your folks handy."

"Why on earth would you want to see their picture now?" Shaking his head Roger got to his feet and headed into the bedroom. He returned with a small framed picture and handed it to Corrine.

"I believe this picture of Mom and Dad was taken about a year before my sister Elena was born."

"OH my God! Oh my God!" Corrine said inaudibly. "It was them! They were at our wedding. Oh my God! The man and woman were the spitting image of Roger's folks and the little girl must have been Elena, Roger's baby sister."

It's best I keep this to myself," Corrine mused as she glanced about the room at the merry makers. "I know that many of the guests would feel uncomfortable talking of the paranormal and I'm positive Roger would. Perhaps there will be a time in the future when I can share this experience with others, but now's not the time."

Flushed by a little too much wine, she sat there in the din of the party

"What a miracle," she whispered. "Their spirits came to our wedding."

CHAPTER 9

Early Sunday morning, Corrine and Roger drove Helga and Rena to the train station. After the train pulled out, they headed out on their honeymoon.

"I can't tell you how much better I've felt emotionally since we met," Roger said to Corrine. "Every day it's getting better. I'm hoping that my horrible memories of the past have been pushed right to the back of my mind."

"That would be so wonderful. You've suffered so much. You're a wonderful man. You deserve peace of mind."

As they were nearing the lodge where they would be staying, a frightening thought crossed Corrine's mind. "What about that vision I had of Roger in the strait jacket?"

A psychic friend once told Corrine that visions of the future were not necessarily written in stone. Rather, they were just views of possibilities.

"I'm glad of that," she sighed with relief, easing back in her seat. She tried to put her mind to rest. To the steady drone of the motor she mused, "What will the future bring us?"

Roger's and Corrine's five day stay at the Wild Boar Lodge was not only enjoyable for both of them, but therapeutic for

Roger. His horrific memories of the past continued to fade. They spent the days sightseeing, some by car and some by hiking the many trails. Evenings were spent in the lodge restaurant savouring the succulent German country cooking and drinking wine. Without question they ate far more than they should have.

All went well until the last night of their honeymoon. After supper they had stopped at a small bar near the Lodge. At the next table was a British service man, one of the occupation forces. They made his acquaintance and found out he was on leave. When he discovered they were on their honeymoon, he insisted on buying drinks for them. Although he spoke broken German, they were managing fairly well. After talking for a half hour, Corrine and Roger were about to leave when two young men came in and sat down three tables away from them. The two had been drinking and were very loud. They were engaging in a political discussion and although the war had been over for a number of years, they were still lamenting Germany's loss.

"I still say the problem was the Jews," the one slurred.

"I believe you," said his buddy. "Let's have a little contest."

He quickly drew a picture of a Jewish Rabbi on the back of a paper placemat and pinned it to the dart-board with a couple of darts.

"Let's see who can take the Rabbi out first," he said, handing his mate a handful of darts.

The British soldier was instantly on his feet, heading toward the dart board. The bartender, a barrel-chested man in his late fifties, got there first and ripped the offending paper place mat off the dart board.

"Have you Nazi assholes learned nothing from the war?" he roared. "Get out of my establishment."

The two made a hasty retreat.

"Thank you so much," Roger said to the bartender, shaking his hand. "I'm part Jew. My grandpa and my mother died in slave labour camps."

"My heart goes out to you. I think most of us Germans know now what an idiot Hitler was. Unfortunately, there are still the odd ones like these arses who haven't seen the light yet."

"That's kind of a sour note to end our honeymoon on," Corrine said as they were walking back to the lodge. "How is it affecting you?"

"I can think of one way we can end the day on a positive note as soon as we're back in our room," Roger countered, giving Corrine a light slap on her behind.

"I like the way you can turn the negative into a positive thing," Corrine whispered, after they'd made love and were snuggling close together. "Sweet dreams."

Regardless of Corrine's suggestion that he have sweet dreams, no sooner was Roger asleep than he was back in the slave labour camp. He could hear the screams and groans and awoke in a cold sweat. Despite feeling upset, he decided not to share the dream with Corrine.

As Corrine's apartment was just a few blocks from the hospital where she worked, they decided to make that their home. Roger commuted to work.

Things were going well for the two of them and Roger had no recurring nightmares. Both were enjoying their jobs. They were very much in love and delighted with married life.

As the anniversary of their first year of marriage approached, though, Corrine began noticing a gradual change coming over Roger. Although he struggled to stay positive, he was becoming more and more withdrawn.

"Is there something wrong?" she asked one evening. "Maybe I'm imagining things, but you seem less out-going now than in the first few months of our marriage."

"I guess you're right," Roger replied after a long pause. "My past is starting to haunt me again a little. After we met, my memories of the famine and the slave labour camps slacked right off. Now, during the day I try hard not to dwell on all the horrible things that happened to my family and for the most part, as long as I keep busy I manage. It's when I'm sleeping that those painful memories screw me up."

"Have you thought about going to see a doctor or counsellor? There's got to be someone who can help you."

"A month or so after I started working in the garage I went to see a doctor. He said my condition was very common for soldiers who'd experienced a lot of horrible things in battle or people like me who had been in slave labour camps. He gave me some pills and said that's all he could do for me. I took the pills, but got so groggy that I couldn't keep up at work. Besides, they didn't seem to be helping any with my horrible old memories. After a couple of weeks I quit taking them. The doctor said that maybe a psychologist might help me, but I'm really not into that sort of mind-bending thing."

"Perhaps you should talk to some other professional. How about talking to the minister who married us? Would you feel comfortable talking with him?"

"It's an idea, I guess. He seemed a pretty fair sort. I doubt it will do any good, but maybe I could give it a try."

Corrine kept up her lobby. Finally, Roger phoned Pastor Burkholder, briefed him on his emotional pain and made an appointment to see him Friday evening.

As Roger pulled into the church parking lot he was feeling quite apprehensive.

"Good to see you again," Burkholder began, greeting Roger at the church door and slowly ushering him into his study.

Burkholder was a white-haired man in his early fifties. Life had etched many lines into his kind face. Sometime back he had been diagnosed with MS and was now having difficulty walking. Although he dressed neatly, because of his illness he had lost many pounds and his suit was more than a bit on the baggy side.

"You've told me a little of the loss of your family to the famine and the war," Burkholder said. "The floor is yours, Roger."

"Well, it's like this. Before I met Corrine the horrible things that happened to me in the famine and the war were always on my mind and I constantly had nightmares about them. It wasn't to the point that it was affecting my work or the like, but I was suffering a lot of emotional pain. You see, it's been with me since I was nine. That's when we were starving. I have so much hatred and anger towards the Russians and Nazis who killed my family."

As Roger retold the agonies of his past he was becoming quite emotional.

"My heart goes out to you," Burkholder softly responded. "Having not lost a loved one to Stalin's famine or Hitler's massacre it would be foolish on my part for me to say that I know how you feel. In all honesty I don't. I can empathize with you a little though, as I'm part Jewish myself."

"I too am angry with Stalin's contrived famine and the asinine Nazi Aryan superiority bunk that would execute innocent people just because of their race. But try to remember the old saying, 'Hate the wrong, but don't hate the wrong doer.' A lot of people don't fully understand that saying. Let me paint you a mind picture to explain this forgiveness thing as I see it."

"Imagine if you will that those who designed these evil actions as the head and trunk of a huge octopus. Those who were assigned or forced to carry out these evil acts are like the arms or tentacles of the octopus. Now, by continuing to hate those who designed or carried out these heinous acts you may think that you are in control, but this is not the case. The arms are only carrying out the head's orders and the harder and longer you hate them, the stronger their grip on you is. The only defense you have is the antidote of forgiveness. When you inject the forgiveness antidote into the octopus it paralyses it. As the arms have lost their grip on you, they hang limp. Seeing the octopus has lost its power over you, you gain peace and control in your life. If you don't paralyze your anger and hatred with the antidote of forgiveness, eventually the octopus can render you completely dysfunctional. Now you may feel that my suggestion may be too hard for you to implement, but in all honesty I know of no other solution."

For a long time Roger sat there, looking past the pastor back into the horrors of his early life.

"Even though I might not agree with everything you say, I can see where you're coming from," Roger said. "You certainly have a way with words. You've given me a lot to think about. Thank you for your time."

After making light conversation for a few more minutes, Roger thanked the minister again and left.

"Well, how did your talk with the minister go?" Corrine asked expectantly when Roger got home.

"He's a nice enough guy. I appreciate that he's trying to help me out, but I wonder if our talk really helped all that much. What sticks in my craw is that I feel that forgiving all those evil monsters is like saying everything is all right. I mean, all of my family had their lives ripped away from them. As I said, he's an okay kind of guy. I'm sure if I bear down, I'll be able to manage on my own."

In the weeks following his meeting with the minister, Roger spent a lot of time in thought. "I know I've got to try not to let my bad memories control my life, but to forgive the bastards who murdered my dad, my mom and my grandpa is a 'no go.' I could never go for that. Still, I owe it to Corrine's and my marriage not to let the past control me."

"Lately, I've noticed you're much more positive," Corrine commented one evening. "Maybe your talk with the minister did help."

"I can't say one way or the other. What it did do for sure was make me realize how important it is for me to try to stay as positive as I can for both of us."

CHAPTER 10

For their anniversary, Corrine and Roger went back to the Wild Boar Lodge for a week's holiday.

"Thank you for the extra effort you're making in remaining positive, dear," Corrine said over supper one evening. "I know you're really working at it. Speaking of positives, I'm not sure yet, but there's a good possibility that there might be a baby on the way. My period is a week late. I've made an appointment to see Doctor Weidman next week."

"That would be wonderful if you are," Roger replied reaching over and taking Corrine's hand. "Have I ever told you you're the best thing that ever happened to me?"

"A few times I guess, but I never tire of hearing it. It's odd, but all day I've had this strong premonition that I am pregnant and that our baby will be a girl."

Corrine saw Doctor Weidman the following week. He told her he'd have the results for her in a day or two.

"I wonder what on earth it all means," she thought as she walked back from the doctor's office. "There's my overpowering feeling that we're going to have a baby girl, my visions of Roger's family at the wedding and then my vision of Roger in a strait jacket."

The next day after work, Roger pulled into the apartment parking lot. "Good news," Corrine called out, greeting him as he stepped inside. "The tests were positive! I'm pregnant."

"What a day it's been! When I told Fritz you thought you were pregnant, he said with us starting a family I'd need more money and gave me a hefty raise. You saved the best news for now though," he added, giving Corrine a bone-crushing hug.

"My doctor has referred me to a Mrs Shultz, a local midwife who operates a small maternity home. He highly recommended her and told me that in the future I'd only have to contact him if there were any serious problems. He asked for permission to contact her on my behalf and I told him to go ahead."

Both Roger and Corrine were elated with the news of her pregnancy. They talked non-stop well past midnight about their plans for the baby.

When they met Irma Shultz, both Corrine and Roger got good vibes from her. Irma was a greying, older lady. Corrine thought she appeared quite competent. Without question she was forthright.

"I should tell you that I'm a widow," she said. "My husband died in the war. It's a sad story I'll tell you about sometime. We had no children so I like to treat all my mothers-to-be as if they are my own daughters. I'm pleased that you came too, Roger. By your name, you're not German."

"No I'm of Ukrainian Jewish background. Because I was part Jewish I was forced to work in slave labour camps. I ended up in the tank factory and then went to work for my tank factory foreman at his garage here in Demzig once the war was over."

"Yes, it sure is good the war is over," Irma said, shaking her head.

Once Irma took down all of Corrine's medical history and examined her, Corrine and Roger were on their way.

On her second visit, Mrs Shultz introduced Corrine to another of her clients, Hilda, a seventeen-year-old single mother-to-be.

"It looks like you two girls should deliver very close to the same time," Mrs Shultz commented as she ushered Corrine into the examining room. "I really feel for Hilda. It seems with the influx of young soldiers in the occupation force on the prowl, a lot of young girls find themselves in a family way without a partner."

"Yes, it is sad. It must be so difficult to be pregnant without the support of a husband."

"I was very impressed with your husband for accompanying you on your first visit. Not many husbands do that. I don't want to pry, but the expression on his face seemed so disconsolate when he talked of the past."

"Roger's story is a sad one. He lost his only sister and his dad to the Ukrainian famine of 1933. Because they were Jewish, Roger, his mother and his grandpa were sent to slave labour camps. He's the only one to survive."

"Hitler was such a diabolical animal, as is Stalin for that matter," Irma replied. "My husband was a high-ranking officer in the German army. He was a very kind man. He tried to lobby against the eradication of the Jews and was jailed. He died in prison of natural causes, or so the official line went."

After their appointments, Corrine and Hilda stopped at a coffee shop on their way home. Hilda was dark and very petite. She still looked much the teenager.

"It's not my intent to be nosey, but what is your plan once your baby is born?" Corrine asked.

"I just don't know," Hilda replied sadly. "I hope you don't mind if I vent a bit, but I need someone to talk my problems out with."

"Go ahead. Sometimes two heads are better than one."

"Well, I can't expect much support from family. I only have my mom as my dad was killed in the war. Mom has a hard time making ends meet looking after my two young brothers. I've been working as a nanny and will keep doing that as long as I can. My boyfriend was an eighteen-year-old Canadian soldier in the occupation force. Two weeks after we broke up I found out I was pregnant. When I tried to contact him about my pregnancy, I found out he was already back in Canada so I gave up on it. I don't know, but I'm thinking maybe it would be best for both me and the baby if I gave it up for adoption. I had a long talk the other day with the lady I work for. We both agreed it would be a hard go for me to keep the baby without any outside support."

"I also talked it through with Mom. She said she'd love to help me look after the baby, but with her working and the tight financial straits she's in, looking after the baby or even supporting me and the baby would be very hard for her. Without Mom's help I'm afraid I wouldn't be able to manage."

"It must be difficult," Corrine responded, reaching over and taking Hilda's hand. "I'll help you in any way I can. If you ever feel the need to talk, just drop over. It's only a five minute walk from your place to our apartment."

"Thanks, Corrine, I'll do that."

"I've talked my situation over again with both Mom and Mrs Shultz," Hilda said one evening when Corrine stopped in for a visit. "Mrs Shultz said there are lots of good couples looking to adopt a baby. Both Mom and Mrs Shultz figure that's what I should do. The more I think on it, the more convinced I'm becoming that that's my only option. Part of me feels like a heel, but for the welfare of the baby and even me, it's probably best."

"All things considered, I think you're right. Will your mom or any friend be there for the birth?"

"Mom said she'll come if at all possible. She lives about two hundred kilometres from here. She's planning to get someone to stay with the boys. No doubt she'll come by train."

"It sounds by our due dates we may well be delivering close to the same time," Corrine concluded.

At first things were quite cordial between Corrine and Hilda. With the passage of time though, Corrine began to detect a coolness developing on Hilda's part. Corrine did her best to get to the bottom of things, but the more effort she put into trying to keep their relationship on good terms, the more distant Hilda was becoming.

On one of their earlier visits Hilda told Corrine she was planning on working up until three weeks before her due date. Mrs Weiss, the lady she babysat for, told Hilda she'd take a leave from her job and give her free lodging before and after the birth.

"I feel so for Hilda," Corrine said to Roger one evening. "Once she delivers and her baby is adopted, she plans on go back working as a nanny. She mentioned to me how hard it will be to look after the children again when she's just given up her own baby."

"One can't help but be sorry for her," Roger replied. "We're so fortunate to have each other. Hilda is a nice girl, but she's only seventeen and not all that mature. Considering her age and lack of support, adoption is probably her only real option."

"I can't thank you enough for all the support you're giving me," Corrine said, hugging Roger. "I know you have your pain from the past, but the way you've been there for me, you'd never suspect it."

Four months into her pregnancy, Hilda told Mrs Shultz of her decision to give her baby up for adoption. Although things were still somewhat in disarray because of the war, through the government agency that handled adoptions, Mrs Shultz was put in contact with a middle-aged childless couple looking for a new-born baby. After being barren for fifteen years, though, six weeks before Hilda's expected delivery date, the adoptive mother-to-be became pregnant and the couple were no longer interested in adoption.

Hilda's mother had made plans to be at her daughter's side for the birth of the baby, but was unable to be there because of injuries sustained in a vehicle accident.

Although Roger wanted to be with Corrine for the birth, Mrs Shultz did not allow fathers-to-be to be present with their wives during the delivery.

At 11 in the evening, Corrine awoke with her first contraction. When the third contraction came, Roger drove her to the maternity home and stayed with her through the night.

By early morning, although she was in a lot of discomfort, Corrine's labour was not progressing so Roger left for work.

Just before noon, Mrs Weiss brought Hilda to the maternity home in advanced labour. She was whisked right into the delivery room. A half hour later she delivered a baby girl.

Mrs Shultz ran a tight ship. She encouraged, if not insisted, on new mothers having their babies bunk in with them shortly after birth. She had learned from past experience though that if the baby was going to be given up for adoption, it would be far less traumatic for the new mother if there was little or no contact between mother and baby.

Mrs Shultz always assisted Doctor Weidman in the deliveries and shortly after Hilda was back in the recovery room she dropped in on her.

"Your baby was a girl. I'm happy to say she's healthy and normal. We've talked before about our policy of not encouraging mothers to see their babies if they are to be given up for adoption. Although we can't insist you go by this guideline, we highly recommend it. What is your wish?"

"I guess you're right," Hilda replied disconsolately. "It would make it hard for me to see the baby and then have to give it up. Anyway, how long do I have to stay here? Mrs Weiss, the lady I work for is a nurse and said she could look after me at her place."

"Yes, Mrs Weiss talked to me about that. Under normal conditions, we'd like you to stay three or four days, but with a nurse caring for you, we can make an exception to that rule. We'll keep you here tonight, but if you feel up to it, we could discharge you tomorrow."

"By the way, Corrine has been here in labour since early this morning," Mrs Shultz added. "She's still in labour, but when she found out you had been admitted she told me to ask you if she could drop in on you once she delivered."

"Mrs Weiss is welcome to visit me, but I'd prefer no other visitors," Hilda responded after a long pause.

"I can appreciate where you're coming from," Mrs Shultz replied, stroking the back of Hilda's hand. "My sister was a single mom. I know some of what you're going through."

With two women in labour at the same time, it had been a hectic morning for both the doctor and Irma. Corrine was having great difficulty and was heavily sedated. Right after Hilda delivered, the doctor decided to induce Corrine's birth. At noon Roger was contacted and shortly thereafter arrived at the home. At one pm, after a very difficult delivery, the baby was born.

Shortly after the birth, Irma met Roger in the waiting room. "Congratulations, Roger. You have a baby daughter. It was a difficult delivery so I think it would be best if you give Corrine a couple of hours to recuperate before visiting her and the baby."

"Dear God, I hope that everything works out for all of us," Mrs Shultz thought as she walked back to Corrine's room to check on her. "I hope the doctor and I did the right thing."

Because of Corrine's condition, Mrs Shultz allowed her to rest until three in the afternoon and then escorted Roger to Corrine's room. In a few minutes she returned with the baby. Corrine was still very drowsy, but both of the new parents were elated with their little girl. Within fifteen minutes she was nursing contentedly. The little baby girl was dark like Roger, but had Corrine's blue eyes.

"Yesterday I told Hilda you'd like to visit her," Irma began, when she next dropped in on Corrine. "She declined. She's going through a rough emotional time what with giving her baby up. This afternoon the lady she works for will pick her up and take her home. I know you've been very kind to Hilda and that you're frustrated that she's acting aloof. Give her some space. She'll come to her senses sooner or later."

"Do you have any idea what we should name our little girl?" Corrine asked Roger later that evening when he stopped by again.

"Search me. Didn't you mention some time back that you liked the name Rosie?"

"Well, the name Rosie is special to me. You see, two years before I was born my folks had a baby girl they named Rosie. My sister only lived a few months. If you don't think it strange, maybe we could name her after her aunt Rosie."

"I think it's a great idea to honour your sister by naming our little girl after her."

"Rosie it will be then," Corrine concluded.

On her last day in the maternity home, Helga, Corrine's mom and her Aunt Olga arrived. Olga was visiting her sister on holidays. Both were thrilled to see the baby and overjoyed at how Corrine and the baby were bonding. There were tears in Helga's eyes when Corrine told her the baby's name.

"We have a lot of catching up to do," Helga said after holding baby Rosie for a while. "Things were pretty tense between your stepfather and me after he refused to come to your wedding. I should have lowered the boom right then, but for some reason I didn't. Anyway, things finally came to a head a few days ago and I've filed for divorce from the turkey. The day you went into labour I asked him to drive Olga and me down to be with you for the birth. He refused. When he made some derogatory comment about not wanting another Jew in the family, I kicked him out and advised my lawyer to begin divorce proceedings. We'd have been here sooner, but I lost several days having to make new travel arrangements and seeing my lawyer."

"That's alright. I'm so happy to see you both. As for my step-father, all I can say is good riddance."

"You've been in Canada, Aunt Olga. Tell me a bit about that."

"Well, as you know, I've been in Canada for a few years now. I left for Canada shortly after the end of the war. I'm working as a nurse in an old folk's home in Camrose. That's in the western province of Alberta. There's a fairly large German community in the area. It's a wonderful country with lots of opportunity. I'll tell you more when you're rested up at home."

Once Corrine and the baby were discharged, Helga and Olga stayed another week to help the new mother. Helga brought some old photo albums with her and one evening they all stayed up late looking at the old pictures.

"This is a picture of my sister Rosie taken about a week before she died," Corrine said, handing a picture to Roger. "I think she looks a lot like our little Rosie other than having blond hair, but look at their eyes. Isn't it scary how much alike their eyes are?"

"There is a resemblance and you're right, their eyes are identical."

That night Corrine had a very peculiar dream. She was still pregnant and could see into her own womb. At first glance the baby looked quite different than Rosie as she had blond hair and a very fair complexion. Slowly the baby's hair and complexion began getting darker. The process continued with the baby's hair getting progressively darker until the she closely resembled Rosie. Corrine awoke with a start.

"What on earth could that all mean," she thought. "It just doesn't make any sense."

By the time morning came, all Corrine could recall was dreaming of her little sister who had died.

CHAPTER 11

Corrine and Roger were overjoyed with their baby daughter. Once Helga and Olga left, Roger pitched right in and helped Corrine with caring for Rosie as much as his work permitted. As with meeting Corrine, becoming a father was pushing the old haunting memories to the back of Roger's mind again.

When Olga got back to Camrose she sent them a raft of information on the opportunities in Canada. She went to great pains to translate the written script into German.

Roger and Corrine spent many hours studying Olga's information package. "Canada sure has my interest," Roger said to Corrine one evening. "I don't know about you, but I think we should consider immigrating there."

"For the last while I've been wondering about that too. It sounds like a land of opportunity. Being in a new country may also help you erase all those old bad memories."

For close to two years they poured over the information. The more they looked into it, the more enthused they became with the idea of immigrating to Canada. Shortly after Rosie's second birthday they began making concrete plans to make the big move.

"I should try to visit my step-grandma before we leave," Roger said to Corrine the day they got notification of their departure date. "I'd better get going on my request for a visit right away. It's probably going to take some time to get through all the red tape."

"That's a good idea. Maybe while you're visiting your grandma, Rosie and I could go back home for a few days."

Only a month after making application for a visit to Poland, Roger got notification that he would be allowed a five day visit to see his step-grandma for compassionate reasons.

"I can't believe it went through so quickly," Roger said to Corrine that evening. "I've got one more week to work so on Saturday I'll take the train to visit Freda. No doubt I'll only be gone for three or four days. While I'm gone, you'll have the car to go visit your family."

Saturday morning, Roger was on the train for the trip back to Poland. As the miles slipped by, Roger's mood became more and more morose. "It's almost like I'm heading back into my past again," he muttered.

Cousin Harry met Roger at the station. Roger's visiting permit allowed him to visit in a fifty kilometer radius of Kozmin.

Roger spent a pleasant evening with Harry and Anne. He brought pictures of Corrine and Rosie and told them of their plans to immigrate to Canada.

"I wish you and your family the best," Harry said. "We'd love to go along with you, but as you know the government won't allow that. The Bible says something like, 'whatever your lot in life you have to be content.' Things could be worse here. We still can operate our little farm and certainly have enough to eat. I'll tell you one thing, it's sure one hell of a lot better than it was in the war. Damn those rotten Nazis."

"Let's not start reliving the war again," Anne interjected. "Living through it once was bad enough."

"You shouldn't expect too much when we visit your grandma," Anne continued. "We've visited her quite a few times since you were last here. It seems to me that her mental condition is getting worse."

Anne made sure Roger and Harry didn't regurgitate too much of their painful past and the rest of the evening slipped by pleasantly. At nine the next morning, Roger, Harry and Anne were on their way to visit Freda.

Freda looked about the same. Although not yet confined to a wheelchair, a staff member had to assist her in walking and eating. There wasn't the slightest flicker of recognition on her face when Roger talked to her.

"It must be difficult to see your grandma in this condition," the matron said to Roger when she dropped by. "All we can do is to keep the poor dear comfortable."

"Does her brother, William, ever make contact with Grandma?" Roger asked.

"Unfortunately, we haven't heard from him since he brought Freda in. It would appear to me that once he got Freda in here and got access to her and Jacob's assets he lost interest in his sister. He's not much of a human-being if you ask me. While I think of it, when Freda first came, she had her and your grandpa's wills with her. I have them in my office. I'll run off a couple of copies of Jacob's will and give you the original and an extra copy. I'll keep Harry and Anne posted about her condition. Sometimes these old souls can hold on for many years."

Monday morning, before Roger caught the train, he, Harry and Anne stopped at a lawyer's office for advice. They updated him on William selling all of Jacob's property and accessing

Jacob's investments. After hearing them out, the lawyer read Jacob's will.

"As you're aware, William has full control over Jacob's estate while Freda is still alive," the lawyer stated. "For the present, your hands are tied."

"It would appear that your grandma's brother is a rather heartless rogue, but his enduring power of attorney will only end when Freda dies. Realistically, I wouldn't count too much on getting anything out of the estate. Seeing that William lives in Germany, no doubt he has all of your grandpa's estate there. My advice is for you to access legal advice in Germany after your grandma passes on. Really, until she dies, you can't do anything."

All three left the lawyer's office in a dour mood.

"We'll keep you posted on grandma," Harry said to Roger at the railway station. "When she passes away I'll let you know. I could go back to the lawyer, but I'll only be able to look into it if it can be handled here. If that asshole William has all of grandpa's estate in Germany I won't be able to do much. The whole thing looks like a lost cause."

By eleven in the morning, Roger was on the train, feeling rather low.

"Life's a joke," he muttered. "There is no justice. I'll lay odds that Harry and I will never see anything from Grandpa's estate. If life were fair, that bastard William wouldn't be able to steal all of our inheritance."

Although Roger did his best to be upbeat when Corrine picked him up at the railway station, she detected that he was not quite himself.

"Is there anything the matter?" she asked as they were driving back to the apartment. "You seem a little less enthused than you were when you left to visit your grandma. Is it visiting your grandma or the thought of moving to Canada that's got you a bit off?"

"Maybe a little of both," Roger replied after a long pause. "Some time ago I started to worry about the money thing and how we'll manage in a new country. Then too, visiting Freda was a real downer seeing she's so completely out of it. Harry, Anne and I saw a lawyer about Grandpa's estate and that looks like a no-go. Chances are we'll never get a cent from the estate when Grandma dies. Even though I'm a bit uneasy about immigrating, I'm hoping that once we're in Canada in new surroundings, things will even out for me again."

"Yes, I'm sure your old memories will fade again once we're in Canada," Corrine replied, a look of concern playing across her face.

"Enough of my bitching," Roger continued. "How did your trip go?"

"Our trip went well. Every place we went, Rosie took star-billing. We had a good visit with Mom and my sister Rena. Rena's got a boyfriend who seems decent. Let's see. We went to see Dad's and Grandpa's graves. I've kept the best news for the last. Mom's divorce is through and she's been out a couple of times with Gottfried, an old friend who lost his wife last year. Mom had him over and he seemed very nice. We'll just have to keep our fingers crossed that things will work out for them."

A week before their departure date, the phone rang. "For you, Dear," Corrine said handing the phone to Roger.

"Hartmann here. I just got your letter and wanted to make contact with you before you, Corrine and Rosie pulled up stakes."

"Nice to hear from you," Roger replied. "We'll be leaving in six days."

"Is there any way my wife and I could pay you people a visit before you leave? My back is much better now. I'm taking it a little easier at work so getting a day off is no problem."

"Corrine, Rosie and I would love to have you visit us. We'll be leaving for Canada next Wednesday, but our weekend is open. You'd be welcome to spend the night. Our apartment is small, but I'm sure we could manage."

"Alright then, Elsie and I will get an early start Saturday morning. It's not all that long a drive so we should be there around ten o'clock. We'll be looking forward to seeing all of you."

Saturday morning, shortly after nine, Hartmann and Elsie were at the door. After getting acquainted over coffee, Corrine, Rosie and Elsie went for a walk, leaving the men to themselves.

"Well, I hope things go well for all of you," Hartmann said. "Correct me if I'm wrong, but when you made your last phone call I detected a little reservation on your part in regards to your move."

"Yes, I guess I'm having a little stage fright. I'm just a bit concerned about being able to provide for Corrine and Rosie in a new country."

"I'm sure you'll manage just fine. We've looked into immigration ourselves. If the wife and I were a few years younger and my back was right up to snuff, there's a good chance Elsie and I would join you. How are you handling your memories from the past?"

"Oh, I think I'm handling them not too badly." After a long awkward pause, Roger continued. "Really Hartmann, I owe it to you to be honest. Over the years I've had my ups and downs. For the last while I was on the up and not having too much of a problem. Now with this big change in our lives just on the horizon, the old memories are starting to come back. As I told Corrine, once we make the move I'm sure they'll be manageable again."

"For you and your family's sake I hope you're right, Roger. We've talked about this many times before so all I'll say is this. You have to start forgiving to get your life on an even keel. Try to remember that."

"I visited Grandma Freda last week and that sort of knocked me for a loop, seeing she's so out of it. The matron gave us Jacob's will. After our visit, my cousin Harry and I saw a lawyer regarding our Grandpa Jacob's estate. The lawyer looked at the will and said there was nothing anyone could do with the estate until Grandma died. He said that the chances of us ever getting anything from the estate don't look all that promising."

"Maybe you should give me a copy of the will. I have a business associate who is a good lawyer. He might be of some help when your grandma passes away."

"I've already had a second copy made so you're welcome to take the original. Remind me to give it to you before you and Elsie leave. Nothing can happen before grandma passes on, but it sure would be nice if someday Harry and I could get a little bit of Grandpa's inheritance. If I'm realistic though, Harry and I had better not count on ever seeing a cent of Grandpa Jacob's money."

"As for this forgiveness bit, I appreciate your concern, Hartmann, but you and I have been down that road a number of times before."

"Yes we have. I'll smarten up and slack off. At times I tend to go on like a broken record."

"You said you and Corrine have been doing a lot of research on Canada," Hartmann said, once Corrine, Elsie and Rosie got back. "Could you tell us about your planned move? As I said on the phone, Elsie and I are interested in immigrating ourselves. Our age and my back are factors, but who knows, maybe when I retire in a few years we might consider immigrating. Elsie's sister and her husband went to the States just after the war."

After spending several enjoyable hours reviewing all the information on Canada and discussing the upcoming move, Hartman and Elsie insisted they all go out to a café for dinner. When they finished eating, it was back to the apartment for more talk about Corrine's, Roger's and Rosie's big move.

"It's five," Corrine said getting to her feet. "I'll get started on supper. You folks are more than welcome to spend the night."

"We appreciate the offer, but my back does better if I can sleep at home in my own bed," Hartmann replied. "I have a custom-made mattress. It's less than a three-hour drive. We probably should leave by eight."

"We have so much to be thankful for," Hartmann said as they were finishing supper. "The war was hell. We lost many friends and family, but the world looks much more stable now."

"I hope you're right about the world becoming more stable," Roger replied. A far away haunted look came into his eyes as he continued, "It's strange, but I never eat a good meal like we've just had without thinking of the times we had nothing to eat."

"Hartmann told me of the hard times you've experienced," Elsie said. "Sometimes life can be cruel."

"It's so good to see the two of you getting on with your lives," Corrine added, turning to Hartmann and Elsie. "Roger has done much better since our marriage. A few down times, but positive for nearly all the time we've been together. We're both hoping that a new environment will help him even more. You mean a lot to Roger, Hartmann. You've helped him so much. To tell you the truth, you've kind of replaced the father he lost."

"My dear mother taught me that looking out for others is what life is all about," Hartmann replied quietly. "It's interesting you'd say I'm like Roger's replacement father. From my perspective, the three of you are replacing the family I lost. I wish all three of you the very best in your new venture. Write or phone us when you get settled in Canada. We've got to stay in touch. Who knows, we may join you some day."

As they were leaving, Hartmann reached out the car window and handed Roger an envelope. "Don't look inside until we're gone," were his parting words.

The second the car pulled away from the curb, Roger opened the envelope. Inside was five hundred dollars in Canadian currency.

"What a guy," Roger whispered, shaking his head.

"Yes, he's quite a man," Corrine replied. "It's so kind of him to look out for his extended family."

Roger and Corrine sold their car and gave away or sold all their large possessions. All that they took with them was what they were allowed on the aircraft. They spent their last few days in Germany bidding their friends goodbye. Finally, it was time to leave. Helga drove them to the airport. After a tearful farewell, Roger, Corrine and Rosie were on their way to their new country. Corrine and Rosie sat by the window. The drone of the airplane engines soon lulled Rosie to sleep.

Roger sat next to Corrine and Rosie, deep in thought. He had psyched himself into thinking that somehow, miraculously, once they were airborne; all the horrible memories from the past would be left behind. But there they were, somewhat muted, but still there in the back of his mind.

As Corrine gazed out the window at the top of the clouds, she too was deep in thought. "Will our new life in a new country be the answer for our little family, or will Roger's emotional baggage come along with him and resurface? Time alone will tell, I guess."

CHAPTER 12

At their first stopover in Toronto, Rosie was a bit on the cranky side so Corrine and Roger did a lot of walking with her in the terminal. When Corrine glanced at Roger, her apprehension started building. Although he tried to maintain an 'all is well' attitude, Corrine knew that the pain in his eyes told a different story.

"God help us all," Corrine whispered as they boarded the plane again.

After many hours, they touched down at the International Airport in Edmonton. Olga was there to greet them and helped them through Customs. Soon they were on the road to Camrose, a small center of four thousand, fifty miles south-east of Edmonton.

"I read a lot about the oil activity in Alberta," Roger said as they drove by oil well after oil well. "I had no idea there'd be this much stuff going on though. It's really something."

"Flying for over five hours across Canada I see what you meant when you told us it's a big country," Corrine added, turning to Olga. .

"Yes and there'd be close to two hours of flying to get to the west coast," Olga replied. "Without question, it's a big land of opportunity."

Not only were Roger and Corrine taken aback with all the oil activity in the Camrose area, they were amazed at how sparsely populated the area was and that few roads were paved.

As soon as Olga knew that Corrine, Roger and Rosie would be coming, she did a lot of footwork on their behalf. After getting home and having supper, Olga took them to meet Mrs. Schubert, a widow living at the end of the street. Mrs. Shubert wanted to move into the old folks' home and was eager to rent her house out. It helped that she was fluent in German. Although the house was fairly small, both Corrine and Roger were enamored with it and made arrangements to rent it. They would take occupancy in two weeks.

"I took the liberty of checking for job opportunities for both of you," Olga said once they were back at her place. "On your behalf, Corrine, I talked to Pauline, the matron at the old folks' home where I nurse. The nurse's aid is moving to the States and they are looking for a replacement. I know you're quite limited in speaking English, but you have a fair grasp of the written language. It's a possibility we could check out tomorrow."

"I also talked to a friend who is a mechanic," Olga continued, turning to Roger. "He wasn't aware of any garages in town needing help at this moment. He also added that until you learned the language a bit, working as a mechanic might prove a challenge as all the specifications are in English. I also checked with a friend who works in the oil patch. Although the money is very good, he said seeing it can at times be dangerous work, they'd only hire a person who's quite fluent in English."

"Yes, I can understand that," Roger replied. "Both types of work would be difficult until I get a little familiar with the language. I wonder what other options there are out there."

"Other than going to work for a German or Ukrainian farmer, the only other job I came up with is the possibly of working on the railroad as a section hand. The section gangs maintain the rail lines. Wesley Novak is the section foreman for Camrose. From what I've gathered, around here, the crews are mostly of Ukrainian background. I work with his wife. Wesley is fluent in German, Ukrainian and of course English. I'm told it is hard physical work, but the pay is really good."

After supper, Olga phoned Wesley. She briefed him a bit on Roger and Corrine emigrating from Germany and then handed the phone to Roger.

"What language would you like to use?" Wesley began in passable German.

"Either German or Ukrainian," Roger replied in German. "Ukrainian is my native tongue, but as Corrine doesn't understand it, we always speak German."

"Ukrainian is my native tongue too," Wesley responded. "Let's use Ukrainian."

Roger filled Wesley in on his experiences during the war, his working in the tank factory and apprenticing in Fritz's garage.

"It sounds like you've had a rough time. Those damned Russians and Nazis. Fortunately, I left the Ukraine before the famine began. There is no question in my mind that you've learned how to work. It's strange, but I find that the people from the old country are better workers than the young local guys. I can always use a good man. I'll be in tomorrow morning until eleven, so drop by. If Olga could take a break from work, maybe she could drive you over."

Early the next morning, while Roger stayed with Rosie, Olga and Corrine dropped in at the matron's office. With Olga's assistance Corrine made out an application.

"Olga told me a lot about your training and your work history in Germany, Corrine," the matron said. "It would of course take you some time to become fluent in English. I understand you can read and write some in English. That would be of great help to you."

"Yes, I can read and write a bit." Corrine replied through Olga.

"Your application is the only one we've received. If you're willing to accept the position, I'd like you to start your orientation in a couple of days."

"A lot of the staff and residents are of German background and fluent in German," the matron continued. "I'm sure you'll make out quite well with us."

After meeting with the matron, Olga introduced Corrine to Erich, the lodge's supervisor. Erich was born in Germany and immigrated to Canada a few years before Olga. Conversing in German, Erich welcomed Corrine to the lodge.

By eleven, Roger and Olga were in Wes's office.

"Hello and welcome to Canada," Wes began in German as he extended his hand to Roger. "Olga will help you with the application form. You can start tomorrow if you like. The railroad has a policy of a ninety-day probation period before one becomes a full-time employee. I pride myself on being able to size people up. I can tell you'll be a good employee, Roger."

By the end of the week, both Roger and Corrine were working. Although it was stressful getting integrated into their respective jobs, they were thankful to be employed.

Corrine found a young mother of two a few doors down from Olga's place to look after Rosie while she worked.

Corrine's understanding of written English helped her a lot and she was trying hard to become fluent in the spoken language. It helped her immeasurably to have Olga at work with her and acting as a coach. As much as possible, Olga and she spoke English when they were by themselves.

Although Wesley talked to his crew in English and encouraged them to speak English when they were by themselves, the men most often reverted to their mother tongue. Being able to speak Ukrainian helped Roger work effectively with the crew, but he was not learning to speak English as quickly as Corrine.

Roger's hope that living in a new country would somehow obliterate the horrendous old memories was not materializing. Although he made a Herculean effort to hide it, with each passing day, his mental state was starting to deteriorate again.

It had been the better part of a year since they arrived and though Corrine kept it to herself, she was sure the past was tormenting Roger again. Although he wasn't crying out in nightmares, as he once had, he would often talk in his sleep. A few months back he held and played with his daughter as soon as he got home from work. Now, while he still played with Rosie a little, he seemed more preoccupied and detached.

"I have some exciting news," Corrine blurted out one evening when Roger got home from work. "I saw the doctor today and I'm pregnant."

"That is good news," Roger replied without conviction, giving Corrine a lack-luster hug. "I guess we'll have to start saving for when you go off work."

"I'm sure we'll manage, dear," Corrine said, holding her husband close. "If our finances are tight, maybe I'll only stay at home with the baby for six months. Coleen, our baby sitter is doing such a good job looking after Rosie. I'm sure she'd welcome the opportunity to look after another baby."

The next day Corrine phoned her mom with the news of her pregnancy.

"What wonderful news," Helga responded. "I'm just so excited that I'll be a grandmother again. Keep me posted on how your pregnancy is going. I've also had a very eventful week. Last night Gottfried and I set our wedding date. We're getting married a month from tomorrow."

As with the news of Corrine's first pregnancy, the prospect of being a father again was starting to move Roger into a more positive mindset. The haunting memories from the past were beginning to fade again.

"I'm so happy with Roger's renewed positive outlook," Corrine mused one evening as she glanced up at the sound of laughter. Roger was bouncing Rosie on his knee and both of them were laughing. "Dear God, let our family always be a happy one."

Notwithstanding Corrine's positive feelings, every now and then she'd think of the vision she had of Roger in a strait jacket. She tried to lecture herself that it was just a dream, but the feelings of foreboding often lingered with her for some time.

Both Corrine and Roger were doing well at their respective jobs. With savings they brought with them, plus the money they were earning, they bought furniture, and a small two-year-old car. They had been saving for a down payment on a house, but put that on hold until after the baby was born.

Corrine's pregnancy proceeded without incident. A month before her due date she took a maternity leave from her job.

Corrine was elated that Roger's outlook on life continued changing for the good.

Although the doctor wouldn't allow Roger to be with Corrine for the birth, the nurse ushered him into Corrine's room when she and the baby returned from the delivery room.

"The Goodz family name will continue," Corrine said, glancing down at the baby boy nursing contentedly. "The little fellow sure looks like his dad."

Roger gently laid his hand on the back of his son's head. Although there was a trace of a smile on his face, his eyes told a different story. They were looking back into his troubled past.

"Do you think it would be okay to name our baby boy after my tato? You see; if it wasn't for him finding food for us in the famine, Mom and I would have starved."

"That would so honor your dad's memory. Gregory Goodz it will be."

Over the next few months, although finances were a bit tight, Corrine, Roger, Rosie and baby Gregory were doing well. Saturdays, Roger helped the maintenance man at the old folks' home to earn a few extra dollars. Roger was doing so well at his job that Wes promoted him to the position of straw boss. With the each passing day, Roger's horrific past was troubling him less.

On Gregory's six month birthday, Olga invited Corrine and the kids over for lunch.

"I can't help but doff my hat to Roger for the way he's supporting you and the kids," Olga said over coffee. "I know he's had some down times before, but now he seems to be right on track."

"He does indeed. Hopefully, his severe depression is a thing of the past. I know the old memories still lurk somewhere in the back of his mind, he's told me so, but he's trying desperately not to ever let them overpower him again. I give him so much credit for that. I feel bad that he has to work so hard though. I'm planning on going back to work next month. Gregory just weaned himself and Coleen said she'd be happy to look after the two kids."

Both Corrine and Roger were enjoying their jobs and the kids were thriving. They were also doing well enough financially to buy Mrs. Shubert's house. They took out a fifteen year mortgage and were happy that the monthly house payments were buying them a home.

"We're so blessed to have such a close knit family," Corrine commented to Roger on Gregory's third birthday.

"We are indeed, we are indeed," Roger responded. "Olga was right about Canada being a place of opportunity."

One evening, Roger returned from work looking most grave.

"You look like you've seen a ghost," Corrine said meeting him at the door. "What's up?"

"It's a letter from my cousin in Poland. You remember my cousin, Harry?"

"Yes I remember him. He was to keep in touch with you if anything happened to Freda."

"That's right. Here's what Harry wrote."

Gritting his teeth, Roger began translating the letter.

Dear Roger,

Freda still remains about as she was when you visited her before you left for Canada. Sometime after Grandpa Jacob and you were sent to the labor camp, William wrote Freda a letter. She had already been in the lodge for some time and was pretty well out of it.

The letter was unopened and in Freda's desk. The matron found it and gave it to us a few weeks ago. That sadistic animal sent this letter to Freda with copies of the letters the SS had sent him to prove that he had been responsible for all of you being sent to slave labor camps. This son of a bitch is the closest thing to a devil I know. If I ever get the chance I'll rid the world of him."

Sincerely, Harry

Roger was visibly shaken. Putting his cousin's letter aside and with hatred in his voice he began reading the first letter from the SS, addressed to William.

Dear Lieutenant Lecholt.

Thank you for informing us of the where-a-bouts of Jew Frau Maria Goodz. Our officers have apprehended her and she now is in a work camp. Thank you again.

Heil Hitler

"Here's the second letter. It's dated a few months later."

Dear Lieutenant Lecholt.

Thank you again for reporting on two Jews, Jacob Isaac and his grandson Roger Goodz. As you know, we are doing our best to apprehend all of the Jewish population in Poland, but it is difficult to cover some of the sparsely populated rural areas. The two were picked up and presently are in a work camp.

Heil Hitler

"That low-bred bastard from hell sent his brother-in-law, Mom and me to slave labor camps," Roger growled. "All I can hope for him is that someday he'll rot in hell."

Although Roger was furious, he kept control of himself until the kids were in bed. After they were asleep he ranted and raved for several hours. Finally, at twelve he calmed down and he and Corrine turned in.

Roger tried to keep a handle on his emotions the next day, but he could talk of nothing other than William's betrayal. With the passage of time, though, Roger gradually gained more control and his venomous verbal attacks on those who had so decimated his family were slacking off. Corrine breathed a sigh of relief when the ranting stopped.

Although Roger had outward control of his fury, Corrine feared that he was turning his anger and hatred inward, as he'd often done in the past. As the weeks slipped by, Roger was becoming more and more withdrawn.

"How are you doing with those old memories?" Corrine asked one evening as they lay in bed.

"Well I'm trying hard not to let it get the better of me, but it's a real struggle. The best way I can describe it is that my soul feels tortured. God alone knows how hard I try to block out those memories, but the news of that low-bred animal, William, turning us all in to the SS opened up the wounds again."

"Do you think it's at the point where you should get some professional help?"

"We've been that way before with the minister who married us, and it didn't help. Still, if it gets real bad I suppose I could try again."

Corrine was constantly praying that somehow, miraculously, Roger would be able to come to grips with his past . . . .

The years slipped by and despite Roger's setback, he was still managing fairly well at his job.

Olga took early retirement so was able to help look after the kids until Corrine got home from work. Roger was doing his best to be a good husband and father. Corrine knew he was still in emotional anguish, but thought that for the most part, the kids were unaware of their father's pain. As they grew older, though, with each passing day, they were becoming more and more aware that their father was a very sad, troubled man.

"I know Roger is in a lot of emotional pain," Corrine confided to Olga one day after work. "Even though he tries hard not to allow those memories to impact on the kids and me, it's hard living with a sad man. For a long time I tried to keep it from Rosie and Gregory, but I think they knew something wasn't right with their dad. Lately, I've tried to explain to the kids without being too explicit, that it's his horrible memories that are making him sad and withdrawn. On the upside, it's good that he's still able to manage at work."

"Have you any idea why Roger hasn't tried to get work again as mechanic? According to Wes's wife, Wes is very pleased with his work, but he too wonders why Roger doesn't look for work as a mechanic."

"I asked Roger that same thing a few months ago. He told me that in his present frame of mind, changing jobs would be more than he could handle. Life can be a struggle. All we can do is hope that in time he'll be able to get on top of things again."

CHAPTER 13

Gregory had just started school when Roger got a telegram from the Lodge where his grandma stayed. Freda had passed away.

"She was a fine old lady," Roger commented to Corrine. "It's sad, but we don't have the money for me to go to the funeral. When I last visited Harry and Anne, they told me they'd help with the funeral if I wasn't able to make it back."

Several weeks later, when Roger returned from work, Corrine handed him a letter from his cousin Harry. Roger translated it from Polish into German for Corrine.

Dear Roger

As you know, Freda passed away a month ago. Anne, I and Freda's two daughters arranged the funeral. The lodge tried contacting William, but got no response. William has taken all of Jacob's money so the daughters had to pay for the funeral. When the staff cleaned out Freda's room they found this other unopened attached letter. The letter speaks for itself. Like the first letters, I got someone to translate it into Polish for me. All I can say is that William is one macabre son of a bitch. By the date on the letter it was written a few months before the end of the war. I can't imagine anyone low enough to send a letter like this to his sister. We've taken a copy of the letter and enclosed the original.

As Roger silently read William's letter addressed to Freda, he began shaking.

"My God!" he hissed, finishing the letter. "What a low-bred devil. You'll have to bear with me if it takes me a while to read it to you. I can't believe anyone could be so low. It's got to be the worst hate mail I've ever read."

To my Jewish loving sister:

I hope you still have enough mind left to understand this letter. I have given up hope on you coming to your senses. Be advised I have taken the liberty of selling off all of your Jewish husband's property and was able to access his considerable savings. You should know that Jews are nothing but a blight on the face of the earth. Soon, with Germany's victory, they will all be exterminated. You will not have to worry about Jacob's Jewish grandsons getting the money after your passing. In its entirety, all the money will be donated to 'The Society for The Elimination of Jews'. They work with the army in helping us rid the country of Jews.

Your Aryan brother
William

Corrine watched with apprehension as Roger clenched his jaw and his face took on color.

"Where are the kids?" he muttered, wild-eyed.

"They're at a friend's birthday party. They won't be back for a couple of hours."

"I can't take it! I can't take it! I can't take it!" Roger cried out, handing the letter to Corrine. He fell to his knees and beat his fists on the floor until they were raw. "Why me, why is the universe so against me? What did I do to deserve this? What wrong did my family do? If there is a God, why is he torturing me? Oh God, let me die like my mother, my dad, my sister and my grandfather."

Roger lay on the floor in a fetal position, sobbing uncontrollably.

Corrine sat on the floor beside him, stroking his head and repeating over and over again, "I love you, Roger."

Gradually, the sobbing subsided. Roger got to his feet, sat down at their kitchen table and cupped his head in his hands.

"It's almost too horrible to talk about," he blurted out. "It's bad enough that William sent Mom and Grandpa to their deaths, but now all of Grandpa's estate has gone to some evil outfit whose purpose during the war was to kill all of the Jews. Who knows, they're still probably trying to kill us Jews."

"Oh God," he cried out, beating his fists on the table, "I think I'm losing my mind. All I want to do is end this pain. I can't take it! I can't take it! I just want to die and end the pain. You may think I've been alright for the last few years, but I've been living in hell."

"Thank you so much for not letting your anguish spill over on the kids and me. Is there anything I can do?" Corrine asked in desperation.

"I think I'm losing my mind," Roger repeated time and time again. "Why was I born? Why was I born?"

He was now hitting himself on the head and his eyes were glazed.

"I'm going to get you help," Corrine said, terror in her voice. She contacted the hospital and advised them of Roger's condition. The charge nurse told Corrine to bring Roger in immediately and contacted the doctor on call.

When they arrived at the hospital, Corrine explained Roger's desperate state to the doctor. After talking with Roger for a few minutes the doctor gave him some sedatives and had him lay down.

"It's critical for your husband to get psychiatric help," he said to Corrine. "He desperately needs professional counseling and perhaps medications on an ongoing basis. We'll have him rest here for a half hour. After he rests, if you feel comfortable with taking him home, you can. I'll give you enough sedatives to last him a week. If he becomes agitated again, bring him in right away. When anyone talks of suicide we must watch them carefully. I'll refer him to Dr. Monk, a psychiatrist in Edmonton. It's imperative that Roger see him as soon as possible."

An hour later, Roger and Corrine left the hospital.

"It's Friday and I don't have to work till Monday," Roger said when they got home. "I'm feeling a bit better, even though I'm kind of spaced out and numb. By Monday I'm sure I'll be able to manage."

"The doctor has referred you to a psychiatrist in Edmonton. I really think you should see him."

"Not a chance. They can't help erase the terrible things of the past. I'm beyond any help they can give me. Like I've said to you so many times before, 'Life's a bitch and then you die.'"

The next two weeks were very difficult for Roger and Corrine. Monday, Roger went back to work and opted to go off his medications. He was very depressed, but as before, attempted not to show his pain to the kids. They soon picked up on it though.

Roger adamantly refused to see a psychologist or psychiatrist, but finally agreed to see Rev. Werner, the local Lutheran minister. The minister spoke fluent German. Corrine made an appointment for Roger and herself to see Werner and two days later they dropped in on the pastor.

In an emotional, tearful out-pouring, Roger laid bare his soul. After hearing him out, the minister reached over and placed a hand on Roger's shoulder.

"I'm not a professional counselor, but I'll do my best to get you help. I've yet to hear of anyone who has gone through so much pain. What's your position on getting professional medical help?"

"The psychologists are not for me. That's why Corrine and I have come to you."

"Okay then, I'll do my best. In all honesty, Roger, all I can do is offer you my heartfelt sympathy and reiterate what the minister in Germany told you, years back. Only forgiving those who are responsible for these horrible acts will give you freedom. You don't have to forgive these acts of unimaginable cruelty nor should you. I expect you'll always hold these acts in abhorrence, but unless you forgive the individuals who designed and carried out these heinous acts, you'll never find liberty. You see, Roger, until you can forgive those people, they are keeping you chained in bondage. Remember, forgiveness is the key to unlock these chains. That doesn't mean you have to become bosom friends with those who orchestrated or carried out these evil acts, but forgive them you must."

"Never! never! never! never!" Roger shouted, leaping to his feet. "It's fine for you to give your spiel, but you never went through what I did. To forgive those devils to me would be overlooking what they did."

Without another word, Roger bolted for the door.

With tears in her eyes, Corrine whispered, "thank you Pastor," and followed Roger to their car.

There was a dearth of conversation between Roger and Corrine for the rest of the evening.

After agonizing for many days, Corrine phoned Pastor Werner while she was at work.

"I'm so concerned for Roger," she began. "His condition is getting worse every day. I'm just so terrified."

"Your husband has experienced unbelievable emotional trauma. It's wonderful you came with him and are so supportive of him. Unless he's willing to do something about his anger, hatred and unforgiving spirit, though, I'm afraid there's really nothing that you or I can do for him. It's sad that he refuses to get professional medical help, but we can't force him to do so."

"I'm so worried," Corrine replied, on the verge of tears. "He's hurting so badly. He's had his ups and downs over the years, but he's a good man. Isn't there anything we can do? How long do you think he can hold together?"

"There's no easy answer to that. It's conceivable that he could continue indefinitely in this mindset and still be able to function at a low level. It's also possible that if he doesn't arrest the mental agony that he's going through, he could end up in a mental institution. All we can do is sit back and hope and pray that he'll soon reach out for help."

"Now you'll have to watch how Roger's condition impacts on you and the kids. If it starts to get more than you and the kids can handle, you must get professional help immediately."

"Thanks for all your concern," Corrine replied. "I promise I'll be looking out for the kids and myself."

Unlike his past downers, time seemed to do nothing to heal Roger's depression. As he sank deeper and deeper into his self-made hell, his nightmares again ruled his nights. His work also started to suffer. Wes had to put him back to working on the gang again as he couldn't keep his mind focused on organizing the work for those under him.

Although he never was physically abusive and seldom verbally sharp with Corrine or the kids, he was becoming uncommunicative, only talking when someone asked something of him.

"Why don't you contact Hartmann?" Corrine asked one evening. "He's a good head."

"It's no use," Roger muttered. "I'm too far gone. There's nothing anyone can do for me. Maybe I'll be lucky and get hit by a train. Really, we'd all be better off."

"Well, if you won't contact him, I will. He just might be able to do something with the estate. At any rate, he'll want to know how you're doing."

Corrine was working afternoons, so the next morning she made copies of the letters William sent to Freda. She mailed them to Hartmann with a covering letter. Making allowances for the difference in time, she contacted Hartmann by phone.

"Roger is not doing well," Corrine began. She then gave him an overview of the letters she was sending. "I don't know if there is anything you can do, but I'm desperate. Roger has never been this low before."

"I'll do what I can. I recognize the name, Lieutenant William Lecholt. He was a hatemonger during the war. He didn't get charged in the war crime trials because he was too small a cog in the scheme of things. I'll see what can be done. William is the owner of a company that has done a lot of post-war reconstruction work. My heart goes out to Roger, but until he deals with all the crap in his past, there's nothing any of us can do for him. I know from experience with my dad. Stay in touch."

Corrine's and Roger's intimate life, which up until now had been good, was also suffering as impotency raised its ugly head. Roger was unwilling to seek medical help and resolved the issue by not only cutting off all sexual contact with his wife, but all intimacies.

As the months slipped by, Corrine became more and more desperate.

"Both the kids and I are being so negatively affected by Roger's mental condition," she confided in Olga one day. "I feel so alone. I don't know how much more of this we can take. I'm getting close to the breaking point."

"All I can do is pray for your family," Olga replied. "Until Roger reaches out for help, I think that's all any of us can do."

"We've got to talk," Corrine began one night when she and Roger were in bed. "I'm close to the end of my tether with your silent stuff and so are the kids. Both of the kids were crying today about you never talking to us."

Roger started to shake. Corrine reached over to comfort him, but he pushed her hand away. Without saying a word, he crawled out of bed and went to lie on the couch in the front room. Corrine thought of following him, but decided against it. She cried herself to sleep.

Over the next few weeks, Corrine desperately tried to keep her peace. When she couldn't stand the pressure any more, she'd say a few words to Roger about his deteriorating condition. He would rarely reply, but if he did it would be to rant and rave in a fit of anger for a minute or two about what William had done or the horrible atrocities the Russians and

Nazis had committed against his family. After his ranting, he'd fall silent again.

Olga was Corrine's solace, but the more they talked about Roger's condition, the more hopeless it seemed.

CHAPTER 14

One of Corrine's co-workers told her that Erich, their supervisor, was very supportive of staff with personal problems. Although at work Corrine occasionally had contact with Erich, she was reticent to make her marital problems known in her work-place. Finally, when the pressure was becoming unbearable, Corrine asked Erich if she could see him at the end of her shift.

Erich was in his late-forties, of average build, balding and starting to get a bit of a paunch. Although he had a weak face, many of the women he worked with thought him handsome. He found that when any of the female staff were experiencing personnel difficulties, having a sympathetic ear not only was good public relations, but would occasionally earn him some fringe benefits.

"Would it be possible for us to talk in German?" Corrine asked when they met after work in Erich's office. "I can get by in English, but I'm much more comfortable in my mother tongue."

"I'd be happy to. As you know, German is also my mother tongue. I'm actually more comfortable speaking German myself."

Corrine was relieved that Erich appeared both approachable and sympathetic to her plight. They talked in great depth about Corrine's troubled marriage. As the weeks passed, Corrine dropped in on Erich a number of times. His caring approach was very comforting to her and as they continued seeing each other, she found the pressure of coping with Roger was easing. The more they interfaced though, the more attracted she was becoming to him. On one of their visits, Erich confided to Corrine that his marriage was also in crisis.

"I'm close to the end of my rope with Lily. She's so cold and self-centered."

Corrine nodded her head in sympathy, but made no reply.

Although Corrine was finding her talks with Erich quite helpful, sharing her marital problems with another man left her feeling uneasy. For now, she decided not to tell Olga about their talks.

After getting off shift one afternoon, Corrine dropped in on Erich. She was in tears as she talked of her marital problems.

"You don't know how lonely it is sleeping with a man who never touches me," she finally blurted out.

Suddenly, Erich had his arms around Corrine and was kissing her neck. He slipped his hand up under the back of her sweater.

"We shouldn't be doing this," Corrine whispered hoarsely as she pushed Erich's hand away. "Remember we're both married."

"I know, but we both have dysfunctional marriages. We need each other so badly," he moaned, again holding Corrine close.

Corrine momentarily resisted, but Erich persisted. Again his hand was under her sweater. This time she didn't stop Erich's advances. Erich locked the door and turned down the lights. He led Corrine to a small cot in the back of his office separated from the rest of the room by a curtain. Corrine half-heartedly resisted his advances, but soon they were on the cot, making passionate love.

"I feel so guilty over what we've just done," Corrine blurted out as she and Erich sat in Erich's dark office. "We're both still married. What about Roger and your wife? How on earth is this going to work out with them?"

"That's a hard one to give an answer to. Roger has problems with depression, I'll grant him that, but in the bigger picture, from what I've seen and what you've told me, the way he treats you and the kids is doing you all damage. Sooner or later, for both your and the kid's good, you'll have to make a decision on whether or not you'll stay with him."

"As for my wife, you can't believe how cold she is. I'm sure Lily could sit on a pile of ice cubes for a week without melting one of them."

It had been three months since Corrine and Erich started having their talks. This was their first intimate encounter.

"That was just beautiful," Erich sighed to Corrine as they hurriedly headed out the door.

"I wonder how I'll be able to live with the guilt of being unfaithful to Roger," Corrine thought as she headed home.

A couple of months passed and although the guilt was always there for Corrine, every week or so she and Erich still had their intimate rendezvous.

"I'm sure no one is aware of Erich's and my relationship," Corrine thought as she walked to work one morning. "Still, how long will it be before Roger starts clueing in? Since that last letter from his cousin Harry, he's become such a suspicious person. It's getting harder and harder for me to cover up. The last time we were together, Erich said he'd think things through. When we meet tonight, we've got to talk more about how it will all work out."

Later, when they met, Corrine held Erich close and whispered. "Remember, you promised last week we'd talk about our future the next time we were together. It's getting too risky. I can't help but think it's only a matter of time before Roger or someone on the staff start clueing in."

"We'll talk about it once we're relaxed," Erich responded with a grin as he pulled Corrine down on the cot beside him.

"Over the last while I've spent a lot of time trying to figure out which way you and I should go," Corrine said after they had dressed. "You say that you're miserable with your wife too. We love each other, so what are your thoughts on us divorcing our spouses and getting married?"

"I've given it a lot of thought myself and though I love you dearly, we both have to evaluate our situation very carefully. What damage would a divorce do to our children and what damage would it do our careers? We have to remember that this is a church-run old folks' home and they may not be kindly disposed to us breaking up two families."

"Are you saying that getting together with me is out of the question for you?" Corrine asked in dismay, a sick feeling enveloping her.

"I'm not saying anything of the kind, dear. You know I love you. What I'm saying is we really have to think it through. I recognize we've got to resolve things pretty soon. I know you feel uneasy about us seeing each other this way. I promise to have an answer for you the next time we meet. Remember, I long to spend the rest of my life with you."

Corrine left the old folks' home in a daze. It was a cold night in mid-January with a stiff wind from the north-east. As she walked the three blocks home she was trying not to panic.

"Dear God, what have I got myself into? I thought things were coming together for Erich and me, but now it looks like there's a roadblock ahead."

Roger was already at home when Corrine stepped into the kitchen. As Corrine took off her scarf and coat and hung them up, she felt ill-at-ease.

"You're late again," Roger muttered, without looking up from his paper.

"The night shift was late," Corrine quickly replied with trepidation. "I know it's seven o'clock. Why couldn't you have started on supper?"

Roger shook his head without replying and again buried himself in Vesnik, a Ukrainian newspaper.

"Where are Rosie and Gregory?"

"Some church thing with Mrs Bernard," Roger said, glancing up from his reading.

"Oh good grief, that will be the practice for the kid's church choir on Sunday. It completely slipped my mind."

"Did you give them anything to eat?"

"Bread and honey and some milk."

While she scurried around the kitchen preparing supper, Corrine was feeling rotten. She always felt that way when she was with Roger after an intimate encounter with Erich. Rodger continued reading his paper and as usual they ate supper in silence.

Corrine glanced across the table at Roger. Pain was etched on his face.

"That look of pain was there when we met," she mused, "only now it's much more pronounced. Dear God, there were all those good years at the start of our relationship with only a few downtimes. Why oh why did the depression have to return? Why won't he try to get help?"

They briefly made eye contact. Her feelings of pity and concern were quickly overpowered by a rush of guilt as her intimate encounter with Erich came to mind again.

As usual, Roger turned in early. Once the kids returned and were in bed, Corrine retired. She was grateful that there would be no intimacy. She was unable to sleep for several hours. She lay there trying desperately to figure a way out of the maze she was in.

Like so many nights since the war, Roger had several nightmares, calling out in his native Ukrainian and occasionally crying in his sleep.

Corrine was up with Roger at seven to make him breakfast. With a heavy heart she watched his car head toward the railroad section office.

"He should be working as a mechanic again," Corrine muttered. "Why can't he get his thinking straight?"

Long after Roger left for work, Corrine sat in a daze. She was feeling so down that she phoned the old folks' home to tell them she'd be a couple of hours late. She then phoned Olga and told her that she'd see the kids off to school.

As soon as the kids were on their way, Corrine dropped in on Olga.

"I'm in a real bind," Corrine began over a cup of tea. "I'm just so confused. For the life of me I can't figure it all out. I used to love Roger dearly, but what with the depression and his shutting himself off from me and the kids, I'm not sure anymore. It seems every day he becomes more distant."

"I've told you before how sorry I feel for you and the kids. It's awful what all of you are going through. Everyone I've talked to who knows you and Roger feels you've gone the extra mile. We all know what the famine and war did to him, but I sometimes wonder if you go too far. Really, even though he keeps a job, Roger's mind is not right. Maybe that's not his fault, but still, if this keeps up, you'll go under too. On top of it all, it's bad for the kids."

"I have the same worries. Gregory and Rosie are so confused with their dad. To complicate things, I'm in love with another man. He says he loves me too, but now it sounds like he's having second thoughts whether or not he wants to divorce his wife. If he and I don't get divorced though, I'll be in a real pickle. Camrose is pretty small. I'm afraid that sooner or later, word will get out about our affair."

"I hope I'm wrong, but you wouldn't be seeing Erich at the home would you?"

"Oh my God, how did you find out?" Corrine gasped.

"Lily, Erich's wife was talking to Megan and Megan told me. Lilly didn't mention the name of the other woman, but said she was sure her husband was seeing someone. Had I known you were seeing Erich I'd have warned you about him. I know him from work. He has the reputation of being a real womanizer. I know for a fact that over the years I worked there, he's had several short-lived affairs with some of the staff. According to his wife, after he has his flings, he always comes slinking back. Lily told Megan she'd have given him the boot a long time ago, but has held off for the sake of their kids. Years ago at a Christmas party he was feeling no pain and the disgusting animal even made a pass at me. That would have been a year or two before you came to Canada."

"God help me. What on earth can I do?" Corrine replied, shaking her head. "Why is everything turning against me? It's hell living with Roger, but at least we're together as a family. Now, if he finds out, it will be more than he can handle. Why oh why did I get myself into such a mess?"

"This may seem harsh," Olga said, getting up and putting her hand on Corrine's shoulder. "I think in the long run, unless Roger starts doing something about his depression, you and the kids might be better off without him. As for Erich, if you go by his track record, he's nothing but a rotter."

Corrine left Olga's place with a heavy heart and headed for work. When she stopped in to see Erich at the end of her shift he was quite uptight.

"Stories are going around that you're having an affair," Corrine began. "Your wife told Megan she's suspicious that you're up to something and Megan in turn told my Aunt Olga. I think we're both in trouble. You could of course do the honorable thing, come out in the open and we could go the divorce route like I suggested last night. I'm worried sick about it all. What if Roger finds out? He's become such a loose cannon, I can't predict what he'd do. For sure, I know he'd pull up stakes and leave me and the kids."

"Yeah, we're in real grief all right," Erich replied without making eye contact. "I got the fifth degree from the wife last night. She's on to me. Someone at work squealed on us I guess. She gave me an ultimatum. Unless we call things off, she'll sue me for divorce and go to my employer. I'm kind of in a tough spot with them. I had some problems a while back and I'm still on probation."

"Was the problem over another woman?"

"Yes, I suppose so," Erich mumbled, keeping his eyes on the floor.

"So what does that mean for us and where does that leave me? I need a straight answer and I need it now. Are you prepared to leave your wife for me, Erich?"

"Could you give me a bit more time to think it out?"

"You've got to make up your mind now, Erich. There's too much at stake for me. I have a strange feeling you've already made up your mind. What's your answer? I have to know now."

"Well, for now I guess I can't go the divorce route," Erich replied, still looking at his feet. "Just as long as we're very circumspect and meet somewhere else, though, I don't see why we still can't continue to see each other."

"I can't believe my ears," Corrine spat out, on the verge of tears. "You really could care less for my welfare. You don't want me for your wife. It's as obvious as the nose on your face that all you want me for is someone to have sex with when the urge comes. I'll never touch you again as long as I live. I pity your poor wife."

"Can't we talk?" Erich pleaded as Corrine got up to leave.

"You've made your choice," Corrine said after collecting herself. "There's nothing more to talk about. All we can hope for is that it doesn't become the talk of the town. Unfortunately, I misread you badly. I thought you were a man, but I see now that you have no spine."

Erich sat in shock, but made no reply.

With tears running down her cheeks, Corrine started for home. She stopped at Olga's place to pick up Gregory and Rosie. The kids were in the front room watching cartoons.

"Correct me if I'm wrong, but you look like you've had a rough day," Olga said as they were having tea.

"Yes it's been quite a day alright," Corrine said, fighting hard for control. "It seems that everything is falling down around my ears. I'm hurting so much, so disappointed. You were dead on about Erich being a rotter. He's weaseled out of his commitment to me like he did with all his other flings. The creep won't divorce his wife, but has the gall to want to keep seeing me in secret. Why, oh why, did I get involved with that loser? God help me. I'm at wit's end. How will it all balance out? How could things get any worse?"

CHAPTER 15

The next few months were heavy for Corrine. Although she was relieved that the rumors of the affair seemed to have died, with each passing day, Roger was sinking deeper into his pit of depression. They got a brief note from Hartmann. His lawyer friend received word of Freda's passing, but was just starting to investigate the case. At this point he didn't know what their chances were of getting anything out of the estate.

On the last Friday in May, Corrine made supper as usual. Roger was always home by five forty-five, but tonight he was late. At seven, Corrine ate with the kids and by eight-thirty they were in bed. Corrine was worried as she couldn't remember the last time Roger was late for supper. At nine, she was just going to phone the section foreman when she heard Roger's car pulling up the drive-way.

"I've been waiting for three hours for you," Corrine called out as Roger opened the door. "I've been worried sick. Where on earth have you been?"

As Roger walked up to her, Corrine could smell liquor on his breath.

"I wonder what's going on," Corrine thought. "Roger never stops for a drink after work."

"You lying bitch," he slurred, poking his finger hard in her chest. "This past winter you were always working late. Well, I found out why. After work, I ran into John, the janitor at the lodge. He told me that a few months back he saw Erich and you screwing in Erich's office."

"Oh no," Corrine gasped, holding on to the back of a kitchen chair for support. "Why, oh why, did I ever get involved with him? It's been over between Erich and me for several months now. I found out he was a real loser."

Roger made no response. He slumped down at the kitchen table. Cupping his chin in his hands he stared off into space, looking past Corrine, back into the agony of his troubled life.

"All those horrible things in my past and now this," he blurted out. "Oh God, I can't take anymore."

With tears streaming down her face, Corrine went to Roger and gently laid her hand on his shoulder. Roger did not move. His eyes did not focus.

"Please forgive me for what I did with Erich," Corrine cried. "I made a horrible mistake. What I did was wrong. I'm pleading with you to forgive me."

Corrine's plea didn't seem to register with Roger.

"God have mercy on my tormented soul," he finally blurted out, shaking his head. "God have mercy."

Slowly he pushed Corrine's hand away, got to his feet and headed downstairs to their spare cot. Corrine followed and tried desperately to get him to talk, but Roger would not respond. His eyes were still looking past her into his own personal hell. When Corrine sat down on the cot beside him he moved away. Weeping, Corrine slowly climbed the basement stairs and headed to the bedroom. She lay in bed, sobbing.

"I know there will be hard days ahead," she thought. "Dear Lord, help Roger, the kids and me through this mess."

Corrine slept very fitfully. Several times in the night she heard Roger cry out in his sleep. As rough as she felt, Corrine was glad she didn't have to work the next day. At four-thirty she finally fell into a deep sleep.

Like Corrine, Roger slept very poorly. All he could think of was straightening up accounts with Erich. As enraged as he was he could not bring himself to take out his rage on his wife. That was not the way he was raised. At five-thirty he got up, dressed and headed the three blocks to the nursing home on foot. He knew that on Saturdays, Erich worked a half day, coming to work at six AM so he could leave by ten. Roger had taken Corrine's keys and let himself in at the staff entrance. At ten after six, Erich pulled up and parked in his stall. He had just begun some paper work when he heard the sound of footsteps. Looking up, he saw Roger standing in front of his desk.

"Good morning, Roger," he said with trepidation, extending his hand. Erich's heart was racing. He remembered Corrine's warning that Roger had become a loose cannon.

Not knowing that Erich was fluent in German, Roger growled in broken English. "I don't shake hands for bastard." Disregarding Erich's outstretched hand, Roger continued, "Go for there." He pointing to the curtained off part of the room that Corrine and Erich used when they had their intimate rendezvous.

Erich shuddered, led the way to the end of his office and pulled the curtain shut.

"Like, I hear you screw my Corrine," Roger continued, his voice rising. "Janitor is tell for me."

"I trust we can resolve this amicably."

Erich never finished his sentence. Although he felt very apprehensive, he was not at all prepared for the right overhand blow that sent him reeling back onto the cot.

It wasn't much of a contest. Roger was no taller that Erich, but built like a bull. He was hard from working at physical labor and fought like a man possessed.

Two of the female staff heard the hollering coming from Erich's office and rushed to investigate.

"Stop the fight! Stop the fight!" they cried. Roger had just knocked Erich out cold and was sitting on his chest, pummeling his face. The presence of the women had a calming effect on Roger.

"Man is bad, bad bugger," he said as he climbed off Erich. "Is have it affair for my Corrine. Is best you take for hospital. I dit know," he said shaking his head. "I go home now."

If the night personal hadn't intervened, Erich's condition would have been much more serious. As it was, he was unconscious for several minutes and one of the staff had to drive him to the hospital. The police were notified and wanted him to lay assault charges against Roger, but Erich declined. He feared to do so would bring his affair with Corrine out in the open and jeopardize his job.

Corrine was sleeping soundly when Roger left and was awakened by the phone. It was the old folks' home with the news of the fight. She was just getting off the phone when Roger walked in the door. He walked by Corrine without acknowledging her, slumped down at the table and covered his face with his hands.

"Your hands are bleeding," Corrine began timidly. "Can I clean them up for you?"

Shaking his head, Roger replied, "Sit." He glanced at his bleeding knuckles and began rubbing them off on his pants.

"I thought I was losing my mind when we got those letters from Harry, but now I know I'm losing it. There's always this screaming in my head and now you and this Erich bastard screwing. What have I got to live for? It would be so easy for me to end it all right now."

"I'm so sorry for what I did," Corrine sobbed. "Is there any way we can try to re-build our marriage?"

"Too late," Roger replied, picking the loose shredded skin from his knuckles. "I can't take anymore. I'll probably be fired when I go back to work and they find out about the fight. I used to be next to Wes on the crew, but he left and now I'm on probation. A week or so ago I hit one of the guys on the head with a shovel when he said, 'Hitler should have killed all the Jews.' Now I'm starting to see funny things. The other day I was sure I saw Helmut coming at me with a club. He was that cruel son of a bitch who killed Grandpa. I swung the crow bar at him several times. When I looked again, I was beating on a post. The new foreman saw me doing it. He knows I'm going crazy. It's all too much for me to take."

"Couldn't you try to get some medical help? There must be someone who can help you out."

"No one can help me, no one. It's too late. I've lost all hope. I've got to leave. I'll send you some money for the kids when I get working again. Last night before I came home, I phoned Wes in Manitoba and told him what happened. He said he'd have a job for me."

Corrine lightly laid her hand on Roger's shoulder. Without making eye contact, he pushed her hand away.

"When would you leave and how will we tell the kids?" Corrine finally blurted out.

"I'll talk to them as soon as they get up. I'm so full of rage that if I don't leave today, I'll go back to the hospital and kill Erich. If the two women at the nursing home hadn't stopped me, I may well have killed him this morning."

"I know you're full of anger. Thank you for never taking your anger out on me or the kids. Even though we're going through difficult times, I still love you and we'll miss you. I'll welcome you back anytime, if you still want me."

While Corrine made breakfast, Roger started packing the few things he was taking with him into the car. Corrine and Roger ate in silence, both of them dreading the thought of the separation that lay just minutes ahead. Part of Roger desperately wanted to reach out to his mate, while part of him loathed her for betraying him. His gut feeling was that too much damage had occurred to the marriage and that now, separation was their only option.

Roger and Corrine had just finished eating when Rosie and Gregory got up. They were completely oblivious to what was transpiring. While the kids ate breakfast, Roger finished loading his stuff into the car and then came back to the kitchen.

"Are we going somewhere, Papa?" Rosie asked expectantly.

Roger squatted between Gregory and Rosie and put an arm around each of them. "Papa must be go," he began, fighting for control. "Like is have it sick head. Always hear scream, scream, scream in my head. Mama will talk more for you. Papa loves my little childing."

"When will you come back, Daddy?" Gregory asked, terror in his voice. "I don't want you to go." The young lad burst into tears, as did Rosie.

Roger hugged his kids hard and then they all slowly walked to the car. Again, he held Gregory and Rosie close.

Then Roger got into the car and slowly pulled out of the driveway.

As the miles slipped by, he vacillated between rage and sadness. At times his eyes were so full of tears he had difficulty in seeing the road. He only stopped to eat and get fuel. When he found himself dropping off, he'd stop; lay his head on the steering wheel and rest for a few minutes. Sunday evening he pulled into The Pas. Wes had a bed ready for him. There was little conversation and after eating, Roger went to his room to sleep. Despite feeling completely exhausted, he slept poorly. Over and over in his dreams he could see Corrine and Erich being intimate.

"Will I ever see my daddy again, Mommy?" Gregory asked the next day.

"I think so," Corrine replied, a sad expression on her face. When she closed her eyes she could see Roger's car pulling out of the driveway and the kids and her standing there, arms around each other, weeping.

"Where has Papa gone to and when will we see him again?" Rosie asked the day after he left.

"He's going up to Northern Manitoba. He'll be working on the railroad. Wes, the foreman Dad used to work for is up there and Dad will work for him again. I hope we'll see him again soon."

"If the kids at school ask Gregory or me where Dad is, we'll just tell them that he's working at a job in Manitoba now, right, Mom?"

"Yes, that would be what to tell them."

"You seem troubled," Corrine said to Rosie one evening, a few days later. "Is it about Dad leaving?"

Tears came to Rosie's eyes as she nodded. Gregory was in the front room, sitting on the couch, half-heartedly playing with his toy caterpillar tractor. Rosie and her mom went into the kitchen to talk.

"I know Papa hardly ever talked to us for the last year, but why did he have to leave us now, Mom?"

"It's a sad story, Rosie. Remember me telling you that horrible things happened to your dad in the past when he was a young boy and then again during the war? I think you're old enough to know about it now. You see, Papa's little sister starved to death in a famine and his dad was shot for stealing food for the family. Later, his mom died in a slave labor camp during the war. Dad and his grandfather were in another slave labor camp and your dad saw a guard beat his grandfather to death. To make matters worse, your dad's step-grandmother's brother, William, is a very bad man and reported Dad, his mother and his grandpa to the Nazis because they were Jews. Your dad was the only one of his family that survived the war. You've heard about the Nazis killing the Jews in the war and the famine in the Ukraine?"

"Yes, my teacher told us about that."

"Well, not only did William turn Roger, his mother and his grandfather in to the Nazi's, he stole all of your great grandpa's money. Great Grandpa Isaac was a fairly rich man. In his will all his estate was to go to Dad's step-grandma and when she died, what was left of grandpa's estate was to go to Dad and his cousin. When Dad's step-grandma died, instead of giving the money to your dad and his cousin Harry, William said that he was giving all of their money to people who were trying to kill all the Jews. Your dad can't seem to get over all these horrible things that have happened to him. In his mind he hears the screaming of people in the slave labor camp. It's worse at night."

"So that's why he screams at night. It used to wake me up."

"Yes, that's right. I don't know if you remember this, but some time back when he was really down, I took him to the doctor, but that didn't seem to help him."

After a long pause, Corrine continued. "There is another reason though. You're growing up now so I hope you'll be able to understand. I'm to blame for some of it. You know Erich at the nursing home. Well, he and I had an affair four months ago and your dad just found out about it the day before he left. Do you know what an affair is?"

"I kind of know a little bit, but I'm not too sure," Rosie replied, shaking her head.

"If you'll remember, I talked to you about the sex thing a while back. You know, when a man and women lay close together."

"Well did you do the sex thing with Erich?" Rosie asked, a horrified look playing across her face.

"I'm ashamed of myself, but yes I did. It's been very hard for me with Dad being so strange and never talking to us."

"Will you have a baby then?"

"No, we used birth control. I told you about that when we talked about sex. I'm so sorry to have to tell you about it, but I thought this would be better than you finding out from someone else. I made a horrible mistake. I thought I loved Erich, that he was a good man and that everything would work out. It didn't turn out that way though. I think it would be best if we didn't tell anyone else about it. I hope that someday you'll be able to forgive me."

"I will right now. I'll always love you, Mom." Rosie went to her mom and hugged her. "I know we'll miss Papa, but maybe he'll get better and come back after a while."

"I hope so Rosie, I certainly hope so."

It had now been a week since Roger had left. Olga was away for a few days and just returned. After the kid's left for the playground, Corrine went over to her place.

"It's all over," Corrine sobbed, as Olga met her at the door. "Roger found out about Erich and me and left last Saturday." Over tea she continued. "Roger got into a fight with Erich early Saturday morning and Erich had to be hospitalized. Roger left for Manitoba later in the morning."

"I hope he wasn't violent with you or the kids."

"Not at all. Not at all. The poor guy is just so hurt. I'll never forget him saying it felt like his soul had died. Some time ago I got him to talk to Pastor Werner, but it didn't do any good. I just feel so guilty and mixed up. Why did I fool around with Erich?"

"It will all work out," Olga replied, placing her hand on Corrine's shoulder. "It may have been unwise to get involved with Erich, but you've said several times over the last while that you didn't know how much longer you could keep a relationship going with Roger. I know he's not a bad sort, but it's a crime that he won't deal with his anger and hate. I'll help out as best I can. With us all pulling together, I'm sure we'll manage."

After she got back home, Corrine sat alone at the kitchen table, desperately trying to figure things out. The reality of their plight sank in deeper with each passing moment.

"God help us all," she whispered, tears running down her cheeks. "God help us all."

CHAPTER 16

Even though Roger's relationship with the family for the last while had been dysfunctional, Corrine, Rosie and Gregory missed him a lot. Rosie was old enough to comprehend why her dad had to leave, but Gregory couldn't seem to understand. Two weeks after he left, Corrine got a brief note from Roger. He'd arrived at The Pas in Northern Manitoba and started working on the section gang. When Corrine read his brief note aloud to the kids, they all had tears in their eyes.

"I wish Daddy would come home," Gregory finally blurted out. "When will he come back, Mommy?"

"We'll just have to be patient," Corrine replied. "As I told you before, Papa has problems with his mind. All we can do is pray that he'll go to a doctor for help."

A month had passed since Roger left and Corrine couldn't have felt more miserable. Loneliness and guilt were her constant companions. She was grateful for her job. While at work, she was forced to keep her mind off her troubled family's plight. The kids and Olga were always there when she got home, but evenings and days off were heavy for her.

One evening Corrine wrote Hartmann and Elsie a letter outlining her and Roger's situation.

As soon as Hartmann received Corrine's letter he and Elsie phoned.

"So sorry to hear of your troubles," Hartmann began. "Even though Roger can't forgive you yet for your affair with Erich, you must forgive yourself. I've been there. You see when my family all died, for quite some time I blamed myself. I was supposed to have been home a day earlier. My wife, daughter and mother and I were to go on a short holiday. I decided to look up an old friend who had been seriously wounded in action and was a couple of days late in getting home. You know the rest of it. The night before I got home, the bomb fell. In some convoluted way I blamed myself for their deaths. It took me quite a while, but with the help of a dear friend, I finally got my thinking straight."

"I'm very concerned for Roger and hope he'll soon see the light. I've handed the wills and William's letters over to my lawyer friend. The lawyer assured me that although it would no doubt take a lot of work to process the matter, there would be no charge."

"Thank you for your support," Corrine replied. "It means so much to all of us."

Once school was out for the summer break, both Gregory and Rosie pitched in to help with the housework while their mother was at work. They were on a very tight budget so Corrine had the phone disconnected to save a few dollars. She phoned Wes's a number of times from Olga's place. She always left a message for Roger to phone her at work, but he never did.

Corrine and the kids wrote Roger a letter every week. Although he didn't reply, every two weeks Corrine would get a brief note from him with a small money order.

By fall things began changing. With each passing month the amount of the money orders kept growing smaller and the notes more disjointed and shorter. Shortly after Christmas, just a money order came. The next month Corrine did not get a money order or note. She phoned Wes again and told him to have Roger phone her at work. After three weeks, he still had not returned her call. Corrine was now growing very concerned for her husband. The day she was going to phone again, she got a letter from Wes.

Dear Corrine

I suppose by now you suspect that Roger is having problems. Find enclosed a money order for $115. A few days back I had to take Roger to the hospital. Before I took him there I had him cash his last pay check and this is the money.

Shortly after you phoned me, he started acting very strange at work. Last week he was working by himself and didn't notice a train coming. He came very close to getting run over. On Monday, when he didn't show up for work, I checked his room. He was in bed and really out of it. He jumped out of bed and came at me with a butcher knife. After I hollered at him, he recognized me. He said something about the guards being after him, whatever that meant. I talked him into coming to the hospital with me and they admitted him.

When I visited him yesterday, even though he was heavily drugged, he kept mumbling in Ukrainian that the guards were chasing him. I'll try to go see him again tonight, so you could phone me when you get this letter if you like. I've enclosed the hospital's phone number. They want you to contact them when you can.

Wes

During her coffee break the next morning, Corrine phoned the hospital in The Pas and got Doctor Brock on the line.

"We've done everything here that we can do for your husband, but he doesn't seem to be responding. It looks like we'll have to send him to a mental hospital. Ever since he was admitted he's been hallucinating that someone's chasing him. Perhaps you could give us a bit of an insight on that."

"Well, he was interred in a slave labor camp during the Second World War. In the past he often had nightmares that he was back in the camp and that the guards were chasing him. He was able to manage not too badly up till about fifteen months ago. Then things got worse and he started seeing things. For the last six months he was at home he seldom spoke to us and always had those nightmares, sometimes screaming out and moaning, or crying in his sleep. Then we had marital problems. He couldn't handle that so he left."

"Yes, he mentioned a bit about your marital problems when I first talked to him. If you could give me the name of your family doctor, I'll contact him and he can get you to sign the necessary forms for committing him to a mental hospital. Unless his behavior changes today, we'll have no other choice. Last night he attacked an orderly. He said something about him looking like a guard. It's just getting too risky."

After getting off work that afternoon, Corrine went to the doctor's office and with a heavy heart, signed the necessary papers. For now she did not tell Rosie and Gregory that their dad was going to be committed to a mental hospital. She felt it was enough of a burden for the kids to be without their dad, let alone having to bear the stigma of him being in a mental institution. Once a week she would contact the mental hospital by phone for an update. The news was never good. On her last call in late June, she talked to Roger's psychiatrist, Doctor Blain.

"I'd sure like to see Roger and so would the kids. Do you think it would be a good idea for us to come see him when school gets out?"

"That would be an excellent idea. We've tried every medication that's suitable and hours of counseling through a translator without the slightest sign of improvement. A visit from his family might just help. If he doesn't show any improvement after your visit, we may have no choice but to give him shock treatments."

A few days after school was out, Corrine, Rosie and Gregory were on the bus to Winnipeg to visit Roger. Corrine contacted Ruth, a cousin in Winnipeg and they would stay with her.

Thursday evening, Ruth picked up Corrine and the kids from the bus depot. Ruth was an attractive lady in her mid-fifties. She and her husband, Gerald, had immigrated to Canada from Germany before the war. Both were gems and made a lifetime practice of showing kindness to all they associated with. After a hearty supper, they spent an enjoyable evening getting reacquainted. In the morning, Ruth drove them to the mental hospital.

"If you don't mind staying with the kids, Ruth, maybe it would be best if I visited Roger first," Corrine said when they got to the hospital.

"That's a good idea. The kids and I will stay here in the lounge and watch television. If it looks like it would be good for the kids to visit him, then you can come and get them."

When Corrine walked into Roger's room, she was shocked at how much he had aged. Although he cried a little when she hugged him, he only responded with a few words in Ukrainian, then lay back on his bed staring at the ceiling. When Corrine talked to him in German, he would reply with a few words in German and then a few words in Ukrainian. He seemed very confused. Occasionally he'd get to his feet, pace the floor for a minute or so and then lay back on the bed again. After a frustrating half hour visit, Corrine asked him if he'd like to see the kids. Roger nodded and started to cry again. Corrine laid her hand on his shoulder, then left to get Rosie and Gregory.

"You will have to remember that Papa is still a very sick man," Corrine said as she led Rosie and Gregory back to Roger's room. "I hope he will talk to you in English, but don't be disappointed if he doesn't. When he talked to me, it was mostly in Ukrainian."

Once they entered Roger's room, the kids nervously hung back by their mom. Roger jumped up off his bed, rushed over and wrapped his arms around Rosie and Gregory.

"My childing, my childing," he cried out, tears slipping down his cheeks. "Papa misses you. Come sit." Roger led them over to his bed and the kids sat down, one on each side of him. "Tell Papa how she come."

Corrine sat across from them. She was delighted. For the first time since they'd arrived, Roger's eyes were focused. For the next ten minutes Gregory and Rosie filled their papa in on the comings and goings of their lives. Roger listened attentively, asking a few questions here and there in his broken English.

Suddenly, the mask again slipped over his face and he began shaking. "I must be tell for you bad, bad story," he began, cutting Gregory off in mid-sentence. "Like in war dem Nemsi(Nazis) come and take Dido and me. Go for Slave labor camp. Is have it some bad guards for camp. Not much to eat, hard, hard work. One guard is bad, bad, bugger."

Roger couldn't sit still. He started pacing the floor, a haunted wild look coming into his eyes. After a long pause he continued.

"One day we go for supper. I see guard is beat on old man. I look and I cry for my guard. Old man is my dido. Dido is have it arms around his head. Dido is say for guard 'I'm sick, can't work like young man,' but guard is keep beating my dido. I scream for guard, you must be stop."

By now Corrine was very concerned as Roger was crying and hitting his head with his hands.

"Dem guard is hit Dido hard for head and Dido is lay on ground. My guard is go for Dido and say for me, 'alright.' I go for Dido. Is blood everywhere. My dido! My dido! My dido! Guard is kill my dido!"

Corrine shooed the kids out of the room into the hall as quickly as she could. Two orderlies heard the shouting and came running.

Roger went totally wild. He began beating his head against any hard object he could find. Corrine tried to stop him, but he was crazed and strong as two men. Roger's face was a bloody mess. It took several male orderlies to subdue, sedate him and put him in a strait-jacket. Corrine, Gregory and Rosie were all crying as they made their way back to the visitors' lounge.

"It went even worse than I thought it would," Corrine blurted out to Ruth. "At first Roger's visit with the kids was going so well and then the look on his face changed. He told us that horrible incident of a guard in the prison camp beating his dido to death. Then Roger started hitting his head. It was just so awful. I tried to get the kids out of his room, but unfortunately they saw a lot of it."

Ruth took them all out for dinner and then stayed with the kids in the hospital lounge so Corrine could see the psychiatrist.

Doctor Blain was a big man with a balding head and a kind, strong face. He had a bushy beard that was mostly white. A bit of the original black color was showing through here and there.

Corrine was looking most disconsolate when she met the doctor.

"I think you could stand a hug," he began, striding over to Corrine and holding her close for a moment. "As I've told you before on the phone, often we have great difficulty in dealing with the patients who are experiencing the type of trauma your husband is having." He showed Corrine to a chair and continued. "As you know, we've been trying various medications on him, plus counseling. I suspected that his depression was related to his haunting experiences from the famine and later the war. The way he acted today confirms that."

"I'm positive our only option now is to resort to electroshock treatments for his depression. We only use them as a last resort. As you may know, the shock treatments tend to block out memories from the past. Blocking out or diluting these memories may get him on the road to recovery. In all honesty, if they don't help, I have no other options left for Roger."

"Yes, I've read some on the electroshock treatments, but do you honestly think it would work for Roger?"

"I wish I could give you a definitive answer to that. To be honest, we're never sure of the results until we use the treatments. That's why we use them only as a last resort."

After talking in depth about Roger's mental history and his present condition, Corrine went back to the lounge. Ruth drove Corrine, Gregory and Rosie to her place for dinner and then it was back to the bus depot. As Ruth bid them a tearful farewell, she pressed a hundred dollar bill into Corrine's hand. Corrine demurred, but Ruth prevailed.

"Last night when I was praying for your family, the Lord laid it on my heart to give you the money. I know from your letters you're having a difficult time now with no more support from Roger."

"You will never know what this means to us and what an answer to prayer it is." Corrine said, trying hard to hold on to her emotions. "You see, I used our last $100 for the trip down here. I have twenty dollars left, but we'll use that to eat on the way home. Our mortgage payment of $100 is due when I get back home."

"And another thing the Lord laid on my heart last night was that Roger will get better," Ruth added.

"I sure hope you're right, Ruth," Corrine whispered as she hugged her cousin goodbye. "I'll keep in touch."

On the long return trip the kids talked at length about their dad's condition. Corrine did her best to keep the conversation up beat. Still, the more she thought on it, the more hopeless their situation seemed to be.

They arrived home late and the kids were soon in bed. Olga was still up and dropped over.

"Roger's condition is far worse than I thought it would be," Corrine said over a cup of tea. "I'm just so discouraged. Maybe I was hoping for too much, but he's so out of it. He only wanted to speak in Ukrainian. I know a little of the language and all that was on his mind was that someone from the slave labor camp was chasing him. The strange thing was that he had a good talk with the kids until the demons from the past surfaced again. He started telling the kids about a guard killing his dido. He just went totally berserk and beat on himself until his face was a bloody mess."

"I'm feeling so down. Doctor Blain, the psychiatrist, said that they would have to give him electroshock treatments. I'm worried because from what I've read, there's always the possibility of some negative side effects with them. That's the only option they have left though. I guess it's all in God's hands."

"Even though it might have been rough on them, I'm glad the kids were with you. Children are far stronger than we give them credit for. It will help you to support each other."

They talked until 1 AM, looking at all the options open to Corrine and the kids. Long after Olga left, Corrine continued to sit at the kitchen table, trying to figure her way out of the mess the family was in.

"Dear Lord, help us all," she prayed earnestly. "We need your help so badly."

Her thoughts kept returning to the debacle she and the kids experienced in the mental hospital with Roger.

"Oh Dear God!" she suddenly exclaimed. "They put Roger in a strait-jacket just like I saw in that vision I had, shortly before we got married."

In the morning, as Corrine and the kids were eating breakfast, both Gregory and Rosie seemed preoccupied.

"It sure is sad Daddy's so sick in his head," Gregory finally said, a concerned look playing across his face. "Why can't he get better? Can't the doctors fix him up? He's been gone for such a long time."

"We can only pray that the doctors can help him. The doctor said he wasn't sure what will happen with Papa, but they're doing the best they can. The doctor told me they're going to try a different treatment on him. Hopefully that will help."

"But what will happen to us if Papa doesn't soon get better?" Rosie interjected. "Will we have enough money if Papa has to stay in the hospital a long time?"

"I'm sure we can manage," Corrine replied without conviction. "All we can do is the best we can. We just have to hope and pray that this new treatment will help Dad get better." . . . .

Back at the mental hospital, Dr. Blain dropped in on Roger.

"I understand when your family visited you the other day you had a rough time."

Roger did not get up off his bed. "Dem Russians and Nemsie.(Nazis) Dem Russians and Nemsie," he kept muttering. Shaking his head he looked over toward Blain. "I tell for you, Dem Russians and Nemsie is bad, bad buggers."

"We're going to start you on a new treatment tomorrow. They're called electroshock treatments. We use them for the type of severe depression that you're experiencing. I'm fairly confident they'll help you."

Roger shrugged his shoulders, but did not reply.

For the next two weeks Roger was given a shock treatment every day. Slowly the memories of the famine, the War, William's betrayal and Corrine's affair were beginning to fade into the background. Doctor Blaine was optimistic for the first time since Roger had been committed.

By the end of the treatments, Dr. Blain observed that there was a marked improvement in Roger as his depression had pretty well lifted.

"We're pleased with how you're coming along, Roger," Dr. Blain began when he next saw Roger. "How do you feel about it?"

"Like, I still remember dem camp, but not as much scream. Is like happen long, long time ago and not have as many bad dreams you call it night . . ."

"Nightmares," Blain prompted.

"Yes, nightmare. Like maybe pretty soon must be go back for work."

"Yes in time, Roger. The staff and I are happy you've started on the road to recovery. I think it would be wise for you to stay here at least for another two weeks or so. If all goes well, I see no reason after that why you can't attempt working again. If you'd care to talk to your wife, I could phone her at work for you. I'm sure Corrine would love to hear from you. Here, I'll dial the phone for you."

"No," Roger replied emphatically. "You talk for her. Like Corrine is cheat me for other man. Must be look after Corrine and childing, but not live for her."

"I think I understand. You're saying you will provide financially for your family, but for now won't be living with your wife."

"Is best," Roger replied, nodding.

Later in the afternoon Dr. Blain contacted Corrine by phone. "I have some positive news for you. Yesterday, we gave Roger his last shock treatment and things are looking fairly positive. He has much improved control of himself. I encouraged him to phone you, but he declined. He's still sensitive over your personal problems. He said he wants to provide financially for you and the kids, but at this time could not re-consummate the marriage."

"I understand. Perhaps in time he'll be able to forgive me and accept me back. I'm so glad he's making a turn around. It would be so wonderful if he could make a full recovery and be like he was before we were married. Hopefully, in time, it will all work out between us and we'll be together again as a family."

"We've talked to Roger about his emotional swings and without question you've experienced them first hand. From what he said, up until the famine he had a happy childhood."

"Yes, that's what he told me. If I look back on all the years we've been together, I'd have to say that he's never learned how to rid himself of anger and hate. When he had his other set-backs he was told by many counselors that forgiving was the only way for him to handle these horrible memories from the past, but he won't have any of it."

"I guess the ball is in his court. Hopefully, we've driven those horrific old memories back far enough for him to function again. Your comment on forgiveness was right on the mark though. Granting forgiveness is the best medicine Roger could take."

In two weeks, Roger was discharged and ready to return to work. Because his work record indicated he was unsafe prior to being hospitalized, head office was reluctant to re-hire him on the gang at his old workplace for 30 days. They would, however, re-hire him to work in Winnipeg on a job where he wouldn't be putting himself or his co-workers in danger if he had a set-back. Roger was eager to get back to work, so he accepted the offer.

The day before Roger started back to work he phoned Corrine. "I'll be starting to work tomorrow so I wanted to let you know that. I'm feeling pretty good and hopefully, in time, I'll completely recover."

"You don't know how wonderful it is for me and the kids to hear you're doing better again. I talked with Dr. Blain a while ago and he seemed pleased with your recovery."

"It's been a rough time for me, but I'm feeling not too bad right now. I'll be sending money for you and the kids again as soon as I get paid. For now, I can't come back and live with you. You'll have to understand that. I'm still working on that end of things."

"I understand. Hopefully things will work out for us. I just want you to know that I still love you."

"I'm still hurting, but it would be nice if in the future I can say the same thing to you. Maybe if things are going good, I could come home for Christmas."

"That would be wonderful. Rosie and Gregory will be very happy to hear that."

As the summer progressed Corrine and the kids were doing well. The financial support from Roger was helping them catch up on old bills and they were able to get the phone hooked up again. They were all looking forward to seeing Roger at Christmas. When school started, Gregory and Rosie were happy to be able to tell their classmates that Dad was soon coming home.

CHAPTER 17

Saturday morning of the Thanksgiving weekend, Corrine and the kids rode their bikes to the city park. Once in the park, they took off on a bike trail. All three were travelling at a fast clip down a steep slope. Suddenly, Corrine's front wheel dropped into a rut throwing her off her bike headfirst into a large tree. Both kids dismounted and came running to their mom's side, but she was unresponsive. Terrified, they started to cry. Rosie finally pulled herself together.

"I'll stay with Mom. You go get help, Gregory."

In short order, Gregory was back with two ladies. While one stayed with Rosie, Corrine and Gregory, the other went to phone for the ambulance. Soon Corrine was on her way to the hospital. Olga was notified and in a few minutes, she, Gregory and Rosie arrived at the hospital.

"I'm just so scared about Mom," Rosie cried. "What will we do if she doesn't get better? Do you think she will be alright, Auntie?"

"I'm sure she will," Olga replied. "The doctor will soon be here."

Gregory didn't ask any questions. He sat away from the others, looking most doleful, tears slipping down his cheeks.

Presently, Doctor Mann appeared. "If you kids could wait here and watch TV for a few minutes, I'd like to speak to your aunt in private." He showed Olga into an adjoining room.

"Corrine still hasn't surfaced. We've just finished doing X-rays and there is a crack in her skull. Originally, we feared a broken neck, but everything appears normal there. It has been some time since the accident and she still isn't conscious so we surmise she's in a coma. We don't know how serious her condition is and it's hard to make any predictions at this time. If she hasn't regained consciousness in the next few hours and if she's stable, we'll be sending her to Edmonton by air ambulance. I understand you've been helping out with the kids when their mother is working."

"That's right. I'll continue to care for them until either Corrine gets better, or their father, Roger, returns."

"The doctor gave me some good news and bad news," Olga said when she was alone with Rosie and Gregory again. "The good news is that your mom is breathing well and her heart rate and blood pressure are normal. The not-so-good news is that she's still unconscious. The doctor said if she doesn't regain consciousness within an hour, they'll take her by air ambulance to a special hospital in Edmonton to check her out. I guess all we can do is wait and pray."

"What's going to happen to Rosie and me and who will look after us?" Gregory blurted out, on the verge of tears.

"I'll come and stay with you guys for now." Olga continued. "I'll try to phone your papa tonight. Hopefully, he'll be here in a few days and then we can make more plans."

When the town foreman brought the bikes back, he spoke to Olga. "It's a horrible thing that happened to your niece, but there is a bit of good news. We've discovered that the hole that your niece hit was hand dug by some scoundrels and camouflaged with sticks and leaves. The administrator checked with the insurance people and there will be insurance to cover Corrine's injuries."

After talking to the foreman and phoning the town administer, Olga and the kids went to her place for dinner.

"I feel so horrible," Gregory said to Rosie after Olga went uptown for groceries. "I like Auntie a lot, but I wish she would hug us a little like Mommy does."

"That would be nice alright, but Auntie doesn't hug people. At least I've never seen her do it. Would it help if I hugged you?"

"I think so," Gregory replied, "It's kind of hard for us without Daddy or Mommy here."

Rosie went to her brother and they held each other tight. They both cried.

As soon as Olga got back, they drove up to the hospital to see Corrine.

"There has been no change in Corrine's condition and we're just getting ready to move her by air ambulance to Edmonton," Doctor Mann said. "Have you had any luck in contacting Corrine's husband?"

"I left a phone message for him. I'll keep trying to get a hold of him. Hopefully, he can come and help with the planning."

After they left the hospital, Olga took Rosie and Gregory for a long ride to help them keep their minds off the awful thing that had happened. After supper, they all went to a movie. Olga phoned the hospital later, but they still didn't have any word from Edmonton on Corrine.

That night, as Rosie lay in bed tossing and turning and unable to get to sleep, she heard sobbing coming from Gregory's bedroom. Quietly she crept into his room, pulled back the covers, crawled into bed beside him and put her arm around him. Neither one said a word, but in a few minutes both were asleep.

When Roger was hospitalized, Corrine made Olga the alternative legal guardian of Rosie and Gregory. The alternative guardianship would last until Roger's health improved.

In the morning, Olga phoned the Edmonton specialist who was looking after Corrine.

"After we do a thorough assessment of your niece, I'd like to meet with you to plan strategy. I understand that Corrine's husband is doing fairly well now and is working in Manitoba. Is there a possibility that he could be here to help us make plans for your niece?"

"I'll try to contact him again tonight. You're right. He's been doing fairly well for the last while and is financially supporting the family again."

Rosie and Gregory were feeling pretty down. Olga felt it would help them clear their minds if they went to the playground for a spell.

While they were gone, she phoned Wes. He went to pick up Roger and Roger phoned Olga back.

"I've some not-so-good news, Roger," Olga began. "Corrine was in a bad biking accident yesterday and suffered head injuries. She remains in a coma. They've just flown her from Camrose to the University Hospital in Edmonton for testing."

"Oh my God, this is all we need. How serious do the doctors figure it is?"

"All her vital signs are normal. The doctor said that in Edmonton they will do a test they call an EEG. He said that could tell them if there's any damage that has been done to her brain."

"The Doctor asked me to contact you to see if you could come home. Depending on the results of these tests, we'll have to make decisions about her care. We'll also have to talk about care for the kids."

"I'll see Wes and get some time off work. I imagine I'll drive. It's only fair that you and the doctor know that even though I'm managing at work, I'm still working on my old problems. I think the doctor thought the shock treatment would end my bad memories. They did help some, but they are still there way in the back of my mind. I'll do the best I can though and be there as soon as possible. Before I leave I'll call you and give you an idea when I should arrive. If you're out, I'll leave a message at the Lodge."

"I talked to your dad," Olga said when the kids came back from the playground. "He should be here in a few days."

"Goodie, goodie," Gregory chirped. "I'm so glad Daddy is coming home."

"It's going to be so good to see Papa again," Rosie added. "I hope he's got a lot better. Now if Mom would just get better."

Monday afternoon, Olga checked with Doctor Drummond, the neurologist at the University Hospital.

"There is no question that Corrine is in a coma. From the testing I've done, I'd describe it in lay-man's terms as a moderately severe coma."

"Do you have any idea how long she could be in the coma?"

"This is hard to say. Usually with this degree of severity I'd say in a range of a few days to a few weeks. Patients whose comas last for more than a month are in grave danger of not recovering. Having said that, there are cases where a comatose person recovers after being in a coma for several years. These are the rare exceptions to the rule though."

"As soon as Corrine's husband arrives, we should meet and plan a treatment strategy for Corrine. Right now we're giving her nourishment by intravenous. You and Roger will no doubt be discussing the welfare of the children. You mentioned that Roger's mental well-being may still be a bit iffy. This is a real concern that we'll have to factor in."

"We will indeed," Olga replied.

"Will he be able to hold together or not?" she mused when she got off the phone. "That's the $64,000 question. God alone knows the answer to that."

When Roger's car pulled into the driveway late Tuesday, the kids were waiting outside for him. After a lot of hugging, they went into the house to see Olga.

"Welcome back," Olga said. "I wish the circumstances were different, but that's life I guess. I've been in touch with the specialist in Edmonton. He said he'd like to see us as soon as you got here."

Although Roger was feeling down with the news of Corrine's condition, he did his best to be as positive as possible and the kids, he and Olga had a good evening.

The next morning, Roger, Olga and the kids were on their way to Edmonton. While the kids stayed in the waiting room, Dr. Drummond saw Olga and Roger in his office. As Roger still had difficulty with English, one of the hospital staff who was fluent in German was present to translate for him. After introducing themselves, Drummond got right to the meat of things.

"We're fairly optimistic from the testing we've done on Corrine. Although she's technically still unconscious, she has occasionally squeezed a nurse's hand when requested to do so. I'm confident that Corrine should come out of her coma shortly. Under normal circumstances she may have some problems with memory, speech, coordination and walking. She may, on the other hand, have no problems at all. On average though, some rehabilitation is usually needed. Rehabilitation can be started in a hospital setting. Depending on the severity of the case, some rehabilitation can take place at home once the patient has been discharged."

"I understand that at the present you are looking after the children, Olga."

"Yes I am. Roger and I will have to decide what will happen both in the short-term and the long-term with the children. I suppose a lot will depend on how long Corrine stays in the coma and what her rehabilitation needs will be. I'm a retired RN so I could help her at home with her rehabilitation."

"I'm kind of overwhelmed by it all," Roger said through the translator. "Olga and I have a lot of things to work through."

Dr. Drummond nodded.

"If you don't mind, Olga, I'd like to talk to Roger for a few minutes by himself."

Once Olga left, Doctor Drummond continued to speak to Roger through the interpreter.

"You'll have to pardon me for being forthright, Roger, but for the welfare of your wife and your children, I feel I have to be. I'd like to get your gut reaction to all that the three of us just discussed. I understand you've had significant mental problems in the recent past and I'm wondering how this will impact on you in caring for both your wife and your children. What are your immediate plans for your family while your wife is still in the coma? What about when she comes out of the coma? I understand you are working in Manitoba. Will you be moving back here to be closer to your family?"

"Well in order to keep the bills paid, I have to get a job here before I quit my current job," Roger said. "Olga has offered to look after the kids until I can relocate. Over the next few days I'll be looking for a job around here and I'll continue to support my family as best I can. The shock treatments helped a lot, but if I'm honest, I still have a way to go. All I can say is that I'll do my best."

"That's all anyone can ask of you. We'll keep you and Olga updated on Corrine's progress. The best of luck to you in finding employment in the area."

Roger began searching diligently for work. His best lead was a Volkswagen dealership in Edmonton. One of their mechanics would be retiring soon and they were looking for a replacement. Roger had worked in a Volkswagen garage in Germany and Hans and Conrad, the owners of the Edmonton dealership, were impressed with his application. It helped that both Hans and Conrad were of German background and fluent in the language. They told him they would notify him in a day or two if his application was successful.

Friday morning, after the kids left for school, Roger and Olga drove to Edmonton and visited Corrine for a few minutes.

Both talked to her, but there was no response. When Olga squeezed Corrine's hand though, she was sure Corrine squeezed her hand back.

After visiting Corrine, they stopped at the Volkswagen dealership. There was good news for Roger. He got the position as mechanic and was to start working in two weeks. On returning to Camrose, Olga and Roger had dinner.

"It'd kind of scary visiting Corrine and seeing her lying there so out of it," Olga said as they were eating. "Other than her squeezing my hand a little, I didn't notice any other response. How is it affecting you?"

"I sort of feel numb about it all. God must have an axe to grind with me and Corrine. First, I'm not with it for a few years and that ends up with Corrine being unfaithful to me. Then I go crazy and they put me in a mental hospital. Now this thing happens to her. It makes you wonder about that saying; 'life's a bitch and then you die.' To be honest with you, I'm getting by, but I'm still not completely on top of things. The universe has got to be against us."

After dinner, Roger headed back to The Pas, Manitoba. His plan was to be back in two weeks.

"I've got some good news for you guys," Olga said, when the kids got home from school. "Your Papa left for Manitoba after dinner, but he got the job in Edmonton at the Volkswagen garage. He has to work at his old job for another two weeks, but then he'll be coming back."

"Hurray, hurray, hurray!" Gregory shouted. "I'm so glad Daddy will be coming back to our house."

"Will Papa live here with us?" Rosie asked.

"Your Papa thought it would be too far to drive every day. He said he'd probably live in Edmonton and drive out here for the weekends."

"I wish Daddy could live with us," Gregory said, a disappointed look crossing his face.

"That would be nicer," Rosie added, "but at least Papa will be here for weekends, right Auntie?"

"I think so," Olga replied, a flicker of uncertainty in her eyes.

CHAPTER 18

For the next ten days, Olga kept in touch with the University Hospital in Edmonton, but there was no change in Corrine's condition. The day before Roger arrived back from Manitoba, Corrine finally surfaced for a moment while a nurse was checking her IVs and spoke a few words in German. Corrine's speech was slurred and the nurse realized she was talking in a foreign language. As the nurse couldn't understand German, she tried to engage Corrine in English. Corrine struggled to reply, but again slipped back under.

When Olga contacted the hospital, she was elated with the news.

"I have a wonderful report from the hospital," Olga began when the kids came home from school. "Your mom said a few words this morning. We should be cautious though because it was only a few words and then she lost consciousness again."

"Do you think she'll get better now?" Gregory asked. "I sure hope so."

"I'm sure she will, but we'll have to be patient. I talked to the doctor. He said although it was a good sign, it still might take her some time until she's normal. She might have to learn to walk again and possibly will have trouble talking. Her memory might also be bad."

When the kids got home from school the next afternoon, their dad was there to greet them.

"I wish you could live with us," Gregory said as he rushed to his papa and hugged him.

"Is best for Papa to stay for Edmonton," Roger replied. "Too far for driving each day. Bad for winter. Like Papa will be come home for weekends. Tomorrow all of us go for Edmonton to see Mama."

At supper, Gregory moved his chair so he could sit next to his dad. After supper Roger sat on the couch with Gregory and Rosie.

"Could you tell us stories about when you were a boy in the Ukraine?" Rosie asked. "I always liked those stories."

"Au right," Roger replied, a smile on his face. "Like in Ukrieen everything is grow it big. Is have it big cherry tree on farm, like tall as three houses. When Papa was small boy, maybe seven, or eight I climb it big cherry tree with thing for pillows. Bag for pillow?"

"Pillow slip?" Olga interjected.

"Yes, pillow slip," Roger continued. "And tie it around neck. And climb up high and make bag full of big cherries." Roger was at a loss to describe the rest of the story in English so he leapt to his feet and demonstrated how he would tie the bag shut and let it down to the ground on a length of cord he kept in his pocket. The bag of cherries safe on the ground, Roger sat down and the story continued.

"My mama is take cherries from bag and I pull bag up again and put more cherries in bag. Baba and Mama is make it pies and have it big barrel and make it wine. And pies and wine is so good!"

"Tell us another story," Gregory cried out.

"Au right. Like one summer, maybe I be seven, I herd cows by village. Other boy maybe ten is also herd cows and find it what you call small bomb? And I and boy is not know what it is."

"Would that be a hand grenade?" Olga inquired.

"Yes, grenade from war long time back. And boy is take it grenade."

Roger leapt to his feet for another demonstration. "Boy is pull it out thing." He demonstrated pulling the pin from the hand grenade. "Boy is throw it bomb for cow. And bomb is go BANG!" he chuckled. "Other boy and I run fast. Cow is blow up and go everywhere. And after, boy's father come and say for boy, 'Why you kill it cow?' And boy is say it 'I dit know what it is I throw at cow.'"

On the kid's insistence, Roger kept telling stories from the old country until it was time for everyone to go to bed.

Saturday morning, Roger, Olga and the kids drove to Edmonton to visit Corrine. Roger, Gregory and Rosie held back while Olga bent over Corrine and called out, "Corrine." There was no response. Then Roger walked over to the bed, grasped Corrine's hand and whispered in her ear, "it's me, Roger."

Slowly Corrine's eyes opened. "Thank you so much for coming," she weakly replied in German.

Although understandable, her speech was still slurred.

Rosie and Gregory slowly came up to her bed. "Hello Mama," Rosie said, stroking the back of her mom's hand.

Corrine struggled to greet the kids in English, but finally replied, "How are my two darlings doing?" in German. She reached out and touched both Gregory and Rosie, then her eyes closed and she lost consciousness.

Over the next few days, Corrine's condition continued to improve and the doctors felt she was coming out of her coma. Although she was only able to speak in hesitant German, she was remembering the odd English word. Within a week she was taking her first assisted steps.

Roger, Olga and the kids visited her every Saturday morning. Olga would occasionally drop in on Corrine during the week. Even though Roger was much closer, he felt uncomfortable visiting her one on one, so never stopped in to visit her after work. Corrine had now regained her fluency in German, but was still struggling with English.

Christmas was spent in the hospital with Corrine. Although it was a joyous time for the family, Corrine noticed that Roger was becoming withdrawn. In the afternoon he took the kids on a tour of the city to show them the Christmas lights.

"I don't know what to make of Roger," Corrine said when she and Olga were alone. "He tries to be pleasant with me, but there's that something that tells me he hasn't forgiven me yet. I mean, how is it going to work when I'm home again? I'm thankful for his support, but I'm so frustrated. I love him and want to spend the rest of my life with him, but I'm still getting the feeling that he's cool to me. Now that I've about got my German back, I'd like to talk with him and see if there's some way we can resolve the past. I guess somehow I've got to approach him, but I feel so awkward about it."

"Now that you mention it, I've noticed that pleasant, but distant manner he has with you. You'll just have to get alone with him. It's the only way you'll get to the bottom of things. He gets along well with the kids now. Because he talks to them a lot, I've noticed his English is improving some. I'm afraid it's something you're going to have to work out with him one on one. If you don't want to mention it to him today, tonight when we're at home I could tell him you'd like to talk to him in private."

Late that evening on the way back to Camrose, both kids had fallen asleep.

"I was talking with Corrine this afternoon when you and the kids were out," Olga began. "She mentioned she'd like to talk with you, one on one."

"I suppose I could arrange that," Roger replied after a long pause. "I'll stop at the hospital after work one of these days."

Although Roger was pleasant, Olga noticed that for the rest of the evening he was uptight.

After work, Monday evening, Roger dropped by the hospital to visit Corrine. She was sitting in a chair by her bed and motioned Roger to the chair next to hers. After he sat down, Corrine reached for his hand. Roger looked ill-at-ease.

"Olga said you'd like to talk to me," he started hesitantly, loosely holding on to Corrine's hand.

"Yes, there are a couple of things we should talk about. Doctor Drummond dropped by yesterday. He said he's very pleased with my progress. He felt that if I had some extra support at home I'd be able to check out of the rehab center fairly soon and come home. Olga has offered to help me until I get back on my feet again and insurance will pay her for two months of help."

"I don't know exactly how to begin on the other thing I want to talk about," Corrine said awkwardly. "You see I really appreciate your support, as do the kids. It's just that I so long to be your real mate again and it seems you're sort of holding back from me. Am I right?"

"Yes, I guess you're right," Roger replied, slowly pulling his hand away and flicking a bit of lint off his pants. "I'm doing the best I can, but it's not easy for me to forget what happened with you and Erich. I hope in time I'll be able to, but it's hard. You'll have to give me a bit more time."

"I'll give you as long as you need. I really don't have any other option, do I? I just want you to know that I love you dearly."

"Hopefully, I can say that to you soon," Roger mumbled, looking most uneasy.

Roger was stressed out for the rest of his visit. He gave Corrine a detailed update on his work and what he observed of the coming and goings of Rosie and Gregory. Both of them strained to make conversation. Finally, Roger left.

In the days to come, Roger thought long and hard on the issue of renewing his relationship with Corrine.

"I just can't do it," he mused. "Nothing has changed. Every time I think about trying to forgive Corrine, all that comes into my mind is this picture of her and that bastard Erich screwing in his office. I can't stand the thought of her whoring around on me."

Although Roger continued to visit Corrine with Olga, Rosie and Gregory on weekends, he did not pay Corrine any more private visits. The pressure was starting to build for him again. He knew he should be renewing his relationship with Corrine, but in order to do that he knew he must forgive her and that stuck in his craw. As the days passed, he was again sliding ever deeper into another bout of depression.

Olga was still living in, caring for the kids. Like Corrine, she knew that it was going to make for a most difficult situation once Roger and Corrine were again under the same roof.

Friday morning, Corrine's doctor dropped in on her. "You've been making excellent progress of late. You're walking and eye-hand coordination is getting close to normal. I understand that you've regained your fluency in German and your English is coming back nicely. About all that I'm concerned about is your occasional headaches, but they too are becoming less frequent. What are your thoughts on going home? Olga says that she and Roger have the house all set up for you."

"I'd love to go home. When do you think I can go? Maybe I could get Roger or Olga to drive me."

"They could, I guess, but I'd feel more comfortable if you'd go by ambulance. Sudden movements seem to contribute to your headaches. You'd have a much smoother ride in the ambulance. We have to pick up a patient from Camrose on Monday so we could drop you off then."

"I have good news," Corrine called out Saturday morning when Roger, Olga and the kids stopped in at her room. "The doctor told me I could go home Monday. They'll be taking me to Camrose by ambulance."

"Hooray, Hooray!" Gregory cried out, running to his mom's bedside. "I'm so happy!"

Rosie went to her mom and hugged her.

Although Olga and the kids were ecstatic, Roger looked tense. "It will be good to have you home," he finally added without conviction.

Saying it was one thing, but his countenance told a different story. He had a tight preoccupied expression on his face and seemed to be miles away. He was very quiet and didn't talk unless something was asked of him. Corrine glanced over at his drawn, sad face with apprehension.

As they drove back from visiting Corrine, Olga was thinking about Roger's worsening mental state. He took the kids to the early show on Saturday evening. After Gregory and Rosie were in bed, he sat at the kitchen table drumming his fingers on the table top, occasionally shaking his head and looking most dejected.

"Is there anything you'd like to talk about?" Olga asked, sitting down across from him. "You seem pretty uptight."

"It's no use, Olga, no use," Roger responded. "I can't handle the pressure anymore. I feel like I'm about ready to fly apart. God only knows the pain I'm in."

Before Olga could respond, Roger got to his feet and headed to his bed in the basement.

"God help us all. Here we go again," Olga muttered as she poured herself a cup of tea.

For the first time since he had the shock treatments, the dreams of his troubled past were coming back. Roger slept fitfully.

After the kids got back from Sunday school, they had brunch. Roger promised Olga he'd phone Monday evening to see that Corrine had arrived safely. As soon as they'd finished eating, Roger left for Edmonton.

"Papa seems awfully quiet today, Auntie," Rosie said as her dad's car pulled out of the driveway. "Is he okay?"

"I wish we all knew," Olga replied, a worried look reflected in her eyes.

Roger did phone on Monday as he promised. Corrine had just been dropped off by the ambulance and answered the phone. She could tell by the tone of his voice that he was on a real downer. He was withdrawn and conversation didn't come easy. With the promise of seeing them all on the weekend, he ended the call.

Throughout the week, Roger was sinking ever lower into his self-made hell. Sleep did not come easy and the closer he got to the weekend the more apprehensive he was becoming. Thursday afternoon he could take it no more. On the pretense that there was some repair work that needed to be done on the car, he approached his service manager and asked him if he could work on his car in the shop on Saturday. After supper, he phoned Olga and Corrine with the news that he couldn't make it home for the weekend because the car needed to be repaired.

Friday evening, the pressure of having to face Corrine had lifted some only to be replaced with guilt over his phony alibi and the realization that today was Valentine's Day. He felt wretched so turned in early. After tossing and turning for a couple of hours, Roger got up and poured himself a double brandy. Shortly thereafter, he fell into a troubled sleep.

CHAPTER 19

Roger awoke with a start. He couldn't believe what was happening. There at the foot of his bed stood his mama. He rubbed his eyes in total amazement. His mama looked the way she did when he was five.

"It's so real!" he cried out, sitting up. "Is this a dream? Is it a vision or is Mama really here?"

"I have come to help you straighten out your life," Maria began sternly. "You're well on the way to ruining not only your life, but also the lives of your family."

"Anger and hatred have controlled your life since you were a teenager. Countless times you've been counseled that you must forgive the past, but you refuse to heed that advice. Right now you refuse to forgive Corrine even though you're as responsible as she is for your marriage breakdown. Don't you recognize the pain you're inflicting on your family? Corrine was in desperate straits because of you and turned to Erich for counsel. Yes, Corrine must take responsibility for her part, but Erich took advantage of her when she was feeling very down. I believe you were justified in giving Erich a good thrashing for taking advantage of Corrine, but now you must forgive him and Corrine."

"I'm trying to forgive Corrine, but I can't seem to manage," Roger replied defensively. "Every time I try, in my mind I see her and her old boyfriend having sex."

"Granting forgiveness has nothing to do with feelings, Son. We'd never forgive anyone if we waited until we felt like doing it. It's got everything to do with taking action. Take ownership for your part and grant Corrine forgiveness. I can assure you that the feelings of anger and hurt will soon be replaced by feelings of love."

"Trust me. I know how hard it is. Before you were born, I forgave your tato for being unfaithful to me. Like Corrine, your tato was a good person who made a mistake. I too had to take some responsibility for him straying."

"I now must show you the pain you're causing your family."

In an instant Roger was looking into the front room of his house. Corrine, Rosie and Gregory were sitting close together on the couch. All were crying. They had just exchanged Valentines. Corrine had made heart-shaped cookies and they were having their own small party.

"I have this awful feeling that something strange is happening to Papa again," Rosie blurted out. "Is he getting sick again, Mom?"

"Why didn't Daddy come home?" Gregory repeated over and over again.

"I'm not sure, Rosie," Corrine replied, wiping the tears from her eyes. "It does seem strange that he would choose the first weekend that I'm home to work on his car. I'd have to say it's a pretty flimsy excuse. It looks like he's trying to avoid me. I talked to his boss. He said he noticed Papa was becoming quite withdrawn. It's hard for me to say this, but

I'm beginning to realize that although Papa loves you two, he refuses to forgive me. I don't think he loves me anymore."

Corrine couldn't hold back the tears. She held Gregory and Rosie close and all three wept.

Instantly, Roger was back in his room. There were tears in his eyes and he felt drained.

"Ever since we came into this dimension, your tato, Elena and I have watched you with concern," Maria continued. "With the deaths of your tato and sister at first you were grieving as any young boy would. As you grew older though, it saddened me to see your grief turning to anger and hate. Your feelings of hatred only intensified when I and then later your Grandpa Jacob died at the hands of the Nazis."

"How can you ask me to condone the murders of four of my family?" Roger replied, his voice shaking.

"We must forever abhor the evil starving of millions of Ukrainians and the mass execution of millions of Jews. However, we must forgive not only those who were forced, or brainwashed into carrying out these horrible acts, but those who planned them. Both Stalin and Hitler have died. I am told by my spirit guides that their souls must make amends for the atrocities they designed, but that's not our story."

"This may be hard for you to understand, but without question, Tato, Grandpa Jacob, Elena and I are far better off than while we still were alive on earth. We're in a beautiful place and the second we arrived, even though we missed our loved ones, we were unbelievably happy and never wanted to go back. If we are all happy, you're having your anger-hatred-fit because of your own loss, not ours.

"For almost all your life you've been enraged at the Russian soldier who shot your tato. He was not a Russian. He was a Ukrainian, conscripted into the Russian army. Horrible though it was, he was just following orders. If he had not shot your tato and the authorities found out about it, he would have been executed."

Maria paused to let her words sink in. Roger sat in stunned silence.

"I'm so relieved that you're all happy," he finally blurted out. "This is almost too much to handle."

"You've heard that old saying 'what goes around comes around,'" Maria continued. "In Helmut's and Erich's case, sometimes justice is rendered in this life, sometimes in the next dimension, sometimes in both lives."

"There is another bit of information I must tell you about before I leave. There is a mystery surrounding William that will be revealed to you when you're able to handle it."

"Before I end this visit, I must tell you that I cannot change your course. Only you can do that. As humans we have a free will. Remember, Son, to turn your life around so you're back on track, you must begin forgiving. That means not only forgiving Corrine, but all those in your past who have caused you pain. It also means forgiving yourself. There's no other way to come to peace. You can forgive Corrine right now. As to the others, it will make it far more real if you revisit the places where these horrible events happened."

Roger shook his head and muttered, "It's all too much."

"Too much or not, what I'll show you now is what will happen to you if you don't come to your senses and begin forgiving." Maria replied. "Remember, Son, because we have a free will, the future is not written in stone. If you have a forgiving spirit, your live will turn around and what you're about to witness will not take place. Never forget:

WE MUST FORGIVE TO LIVE."

The bedroom faded from Roger's view and he seemed to be floating in space. Then he saw the front of a large brick building. He read aloud, "REGIONAL MENTAL HOSPITAL." Instantly he was in a blood spattered room. To his horror, he melded into the body of the screaming patient. It was his old demented self, far lower than he'd ever been before at his lowest. The terrible scenes from his past were flashing through his head, magnified tenfold from the worst he'd ever experienced.

He was screaming at the top of his lungs and beating his bloody head against any hard object he could find.

"God help me, God help me," he cried out time and time again.

Suddenly, two large male orderlies were in his room. Their mission was to subdue him. He fought like one possessed, hitting with his fists, kicking and biting. Then the orderlies had him pinned and one orderly jabbed a needle into his thigh.

In terror, he saw that the other orderly was holding a strait jacket.

"OH NO! NOT THE STRAIT JACKET!" he bellowed, "GOD HELP ME! NOT THE STRAIT JACKET! HELP ME! PLEASE GOD, HELP ME! NO, NOT THE STRAIT JACKET! NOT THE STRAIT JACKET! NOT THE STRAIT JACKET!"

Instantly, Roger was back in his room, hollering at the top of his lungs.

He glanced down at his left hand. To his horror he saw the plastic bracelet that patients wear in the hospital was still on his wrist. In a panic he reached for it with his right hand. Just as he was going to touch it, the bracelet disappeared.

"Thank you God for it all being just a dream," he said over and over again, but just then, something caught his eye.

"What's that?" he whispered.

In the semi-darkness of his room he saw the spirit of his mother moving towards the door. Slowly she passed right through it. Suddenly, permeating the room was an acrid smell that brought back fond memories from his childhood. It was the aroma of mustard pickles that his mother was making. In his mind's eye he was again perched up on a stool in their kitchen, back in the Ukraine. He could see the pot of steaming pickles and his mother ladling the pickles into jars. Roger sat up in bed wide awake.

"How could all of this be a dream?" he muttered. "It was all so real."

Roger leapt to his feet, turned on the light and glanced at his watch. It was a few minutes short of eleven.

"Why, oh why, did I spend my whole life so full of anger and hate? Thank you Mama for coming to me tonight," he whispered. "Thank you! Thank you! Thank you!"

CHAPTER 20

Roger quickly dressed. He was shell-shocked with the realization that his kinfolk were happy where they were and never had any desire to return to this dimension. The thought had never occurred to him before. It gave him such an immense feeling of relief.

"Damn it, what an arse I've been all these years," he muttered. "Here it is Valentine's Day and I haven't had the brains to get Corrine or the kids anything. What an idiot I am, all wrapped up in keeping mad and hurt." As he anticipated making amends with Corrine, there were tears in his eyes. "I can't believe it," he said aloud. "Mama was right. I'm now beginning to feel all the love for her that I've been covering up for the last while. I take my responsibility in our marriage breakdown. Why the devil couldn't I get that through my noggin before? I'll worry about my feelings from the past later. Right now I have a family to salvage."

In a few minutes Roger was in his car. There was a convenience store a couple of blocks from his place that stayed open till twelve. Fortunately, they still had a good assortment of Valentine cards and chocolates. Roger picked up three boxes of chocolates, three cards and took them to the till.

"Running a little late, I see," the lady at the till said with a smile. She had white hair and appeared to be in her late sixties.

"I'm glad you be open," Roger replied as he handed her the money.

"For your family, I suppose."

Roger nodded.

"Perhaps I shouldn't ask, but do you have any flowers for your wife?"

"No, too late." Roger said shaking his head. "All flower stores be closed now."

The lady reached under the counter and brought out a dozen roses still wrapped in cellophane.

"Here, I'll give you six roses for your wife. You see, every Valentine's Day my son brings me a dozen roses. His dad always got me flowers when he was alive, but he's been gone many years now."

Despite Roger protesting, the lady peeled back the cellophane and divided the roses. She wrapped the six remaining roses in the cellophane again and handed them to Roger.

"No, no. Flowers be for you," Roger continued, shaking his head.

"I insist," the lady retorted, "and of course there is no charge. When you came into the store something inside of me said 'give this man some of your roses.'"

"Thank you, thank you. Is never know it how much this means for wife."

Roger was soon on the road to Camrose. As the miles slipped by, the visit from his mama and then the kindness of the lady in the store were so etched in his mind he could think of nothing else . . . .

"No Roger on Valentine's Day," Corrine mused as she lay in bed. "What hurts most is that despite all my wishful thinking, it looks like my relationship with him is over. His love for me appears to be a thing of the past, but why couldn't he at least have remembered the kids on Valentine's Day?" Corrine finally cried herself to sleep.

It was one in the morning when Roger pulled into their driveway. Corrine awoke with a start. Roger was hovering over her, smiling with that old smile she hadn't seen in years.

"Oh my God! It's you!" Corrine whispered. "I'm so glad you decided to come home after all."

Roger flipped on the light, put Corrine's flowers on the end table and handed her the Valentine card. Quickly she opened it.

Dearest Corrine.

I have hopefully come to my senses. Tonight I discovered that for most of my life I've made an ass of myself. I forgive you for your part in our marriage break down. Please forgive me for my part in it and all the pain I've caused you and the kids over the years. Let's start over again tonight."

Love, Roger

In a flash, Corrine leapt out of bed and was in Roger's arms. "I've waited so long for this moment, so long," she cried.

Roger had just finished telling Corrine about the visitation of his mom when the bedroom door opened a crack.

"Can we come in?" Rosie asked hesitantly.

Roger opened the door and embraced the kids.

"Gregory couldn't sleep so he was in my room," Rosie continued, "and then we heard Papa come into the house."

"Come, let's go to the kitchen," Roger said in German.

They followed Roger into the kitchen. At Rosie's place at the table were two roses, a chocolate heart and a Valentine card. At Gregory's place, a Valentine card, another chocolate heart and a toy Porsche racing car.

"We have so much to talk about," Roger continued as Rosie and Gregory were looking at their gifts. "I hope both you kids still understand German. I'm much more comfortable speaking it than English."

"Go ahead Papa," Rosie replied. "Gregory and I can understand."

"I must start by asking you kids to forgive me for all the pain I've caused you over the years. I was so tied up in my own pain that I never realized how much hurt I caused you two. Up until last night I was still mixed up. I had a most wonderful vision. My mama who has been dead for many, many years visited me. I might add that at first it was pretty scary."

Over a cup of cocoa, Roger told of his encounter with his mama's spirit.

"Tomorrow is the start of a new life for us all," Roger said. "Some of it, like forgiving those who killed my family, will not be easy for me, but I swear with your help I'm never going back to where I was. For starters, I plan on moving home next week."

"Hooray, hooray for our side," Gregory called out. "Daddy is going to live in our house again."

Rosie carefully placed her two roses in a vase. "Thank you so much, Papa," she said, tears of happiness glistening in her eyes. "These are the first flowers I've ever gotten. I thought today was going to be one of the worst days of my life, but now it's turned into the best day I've ever had."

"Thank you, Lord," Corrine whispered as she glanced at the glow in the faces of Roger and the kids. "Let this happiness last forever."

"So much to talk about," Roger said to Corrine, after the kids had gone to bed. "First though, maybe we should make up for lost time." He took Corrine by the hand and led her into the bedroom.

"I'm willing and able," Corrine replied seductively, pulling off her nightie and hopping into bed. They were both very emotionally charged and made love as though possessed, soaring to new heights of ecstasy and release.

"That was just so beautiful," Corrine whispered as she lay close to Roger. "I'm so glad we've been given another chance."

"I couldn't agree more. I know it's not going to be easy for me to change a lifetime of hatred, anger and feeling sorry for myself, but I'm going to break my butt trying. If you notice me slipping, help me back on the path again." Snuggled close together, they were soon asleep.

Gregory and Rosie were up before their parents. On Rosie's insistence they started preparing breakfast.

"It would be fun to make breakfast and take it to Mom and Papa in bed," Rosie said.

Rosie had apprenticed making pancakes under Olga's tutelage and was soon whipping up a large bowl of batter. While Rosie worked on the pancakes, Gregory got plates, trays and cutlery. He also boiled some water for instant coffee.

"I think Papa was doing the sex thing with Mom last night," Gregory volunteered. "I had to go to the bathroom and their bedroom door was open a bit.

"Yikes," Rosie responded.

It was providential for all concerned that when the kids got to their folks' bedroom with breakfast, Rosie knocked on the bedroom door and called out, "breakfast." Without question her announcement prevented another 'sex thing' scene.

"What a wonderful surprise," Corrine called out. "Come on in."

After putting all the breakfast paraphernalia on the bed and dresser, the kids brought in chairs and coffee tables so they could have breakfast too.

"Wonderful, wonderful!" Roger exclaimed after finishing his last cup of coffee. "Is best breakfast ever have it for long, long time."

"You're welcome Papa," Rosie replied. "Talk to us in German like you did last night. It's easier for you than English. Gregory and I learned German first you know and Aunt Olga and mom have been talking to Gregory and me in German ever since you left. We're getting pretty good at it now."

After the dishes were washed, they all sat down at the table.

"Thanks for letting me speak in German," Roger began, turning to Rosie and Gregory. "I promise to learn to speak better English."

"As I started to tell you last night, I'm moving home. First, I'll have to straighten up with my landlord. On Sunday afternoon, I'll load up all my stuff and bring it home. I'll drive back and forth to work for now. When my mama came to me in the vision, she told me that things would work out for us. Let's all pray that they do."

"Gregory and I have been praying for that ever since you came back from Manitoba and so has Mom," Rosie said. "Ever since I can remember, we've prayed that you'd get better and not have those horrible nightmares anymore."

"Well maybe God is answering all our prayers. Last night had to be a miracle. To tell you the truth, I'm a little worried as to what will happen to me job-wise. For now I'll commute, but it is well over an hour one way. We'll just have to see how everything turns out."

"As my mother used to say, 'it will all come out in the wash.' Hey! How about us all going to a show this afternoon?"

"You and the kids go," Corrine responded. "I still get headaches if I watch television or movies."

"Maybe you and Gregory go," Rosie added. "I'll stay home with Mom and help her make a big celebration supper. Aunt Olga won't be back until tomorrow so Mom and I can do it."

"That's very kind of you," Corrine interjected, "but are you sure you don't want to go?"

"No that's fine. I'm excited about helping you make a real banquet to celebrate Papa moving home."

After dinner, Gregory and Roger left for the show.

"You must be so happy with Papa forgiving you and him sleeping with you again," Rosie said as she was helping her mom.

"It's the most wonderful thing that ever happened to me. Once in a while I think I should pinch myself in case it's just a dream."

"I can't ever remember Papa being like he is now, especially the last few years when he wouldn't talk to us. You're right, it's like it's too good to be true."

"Yes, it's unbelievable all right. His mother had to talk to him before he could get on the right track and get his thinking straight."

Supper was ready by the time the men got home. And what a supper it was! There was roast pork, mashed potatoes, turnips and parsnips for the main course. Dessert was a strawberry rhubarb pie Rosie had made with Corrine's guidance. Both Roger and Gregory told the ladies that it was the best meal they'd ever eaten.

After supper, Roger phoned Hans, his boss, to tell him of his plan to commute to work.

"It's strange you should call, Roger. I'm having a hard time believing the coincidence of all this. Late last night I got a call from Reinhold Jensen, an old business friend in Camrose. He runs Alpine Motors and specializes in repairing foreign cars."

"Yes, I know him. When we emigrated from Germany we bought our first car from him."

"Anyway, he's sixty-eight and wants to retire. Here's the eerie part. He asked me if Conrad and I would be interested in buying his business. He knows you live in Camrose and suggested that if we took over the business we could get you to work there. He said that one of his mechanics, about his age wants to shut it down too. The other mechanic is willing to stay on. I was going to talk to you Monday about the deal. Up until now I was unsure of your personal situation, but now with you wanting to live in Camrose again, well maybe it would work out for all of us."

"This is unbelievable," Roger responded, shaking his head. "Without question, things are falling into place."

"Well, okay, we'll talk about it Monday morning. If we do buy Reinhold out, we sure want to have you work there. There are some renovations and an addition that needs to be made to his old garage. If we make a deal, maybe I could also get you to help oversee the additions to the garage we plan on making."

When Roger got off the phone he was still shaking his head.

"I can't believe it. Last night Hans got a phone call from Reinhold Jensen. You remember him. He owns Alpine Motors here in town. We bought our first car from him."

"Yes, go ahead," Corrine replied impatiently.

"Well, he wants to retire and asked Hans and Conrad to buy his business. Reinhold knew I was working for them in Edmonton and suggested that if Hans and Conrad bought him out, I could work here in the garage. I can't believe how it's all falling into place."

"Without question, God is answering our prayers," Corrine replied. "First, there's the visitation from the spirit of your mom and now this. The hand of The Almighty is evident."

Roger did not reply. He sat at the table, slowly shaking his head. "Mama was right about things working out for us," he finally whispered.

Sunday morning, Roger went to church with Corrine and the kids. It was the first time he attended in years. Sunday afternoon, Roger, Rosie and Gregory drove back to Edmonton to clean out his room. Corrine would have come, but her doctor didn't want her doing heavy physical labor for a few more weeks. Roger dropped the car off at the garage and picked up a half ton truck. With the help of the kids, the work went fast and by six, everything was loaded into the truck and they were on the road. When they got home, Corrine had supper ready for them. By ten o'clock everything had been unloaded and moved into the house.

Rather than head back to work Monday morning, Roger met with Hans, Conrad and Reinhold at Alpine Motors to discuss the proposed buy-out. After sitting in on their preliminary talks, Roger left for work in Edmonton.

Later in the afternoon, after Hans returned to Edmonton, he called Roger into his office.

"Well, we made a deal. We'll be getting the legal paper work drawn up this week and will take possession in two weeks. If you're in agreement, you could start there tomorrow and get the feel of the business. When we take over, we'd like to make you shop foreman. We've talked to Ernie and offered him the option of switching from service manager here to the service manager of the garage in Camrose. He's accepted the offer and was happy with the prospects of working with you. For now I'll act as service manager here until we can find someone. What are your thoughts?"

"That would sure work out good for me. Ernie and I have always gotten along well so there would be no problem there."

"Maybe you should keep the pickup then and use it tonight to move your tools to Camrose."

By five thirty, Roger was on the road. Reinhold stayed late at the garage and helped Roger move his tools in.

Olga had returned. She was visiting with Corrine and helping her prepare supper. The kids ate early and went to the skating rink.

"I hope you're right about Roger turning over a new leaf," Olga responded after hearing what had transpired. "It's certainly positive that he's forgiven you and moved home. I just hope it's not going to be like the past, you know, 'the old roller coaster ride.'"

Before Corrine could reply, they heard Roger's vehicle pull into the driveway.

"I can't believe all the good things that are happening," he called out as soon as he was in the door. "Hans and Conrad are buying Alpine Motors. They want me to be shop foreman in two weeks when we take over. I'm a bit late because I brought all my tools out to the garage with the company truck. I'll be working here as a mechanic for the time being."

"I'm so happy for you and Corrine," Olga said, after some thought. "I just hope and pray everything will work out for the two of you and the kids."

"I'd like to thank you for all the support you've given our family," Roger said, turning to Olga. "I know it's not been easy for you with me being so out of it all these years. I promise before God, things will be different now. As you know firsthand, I spent twenty plus years in my own self-made hell. I know it won't always be straight ahead for me, but I vow to keep working on erasing all that anger and hatred I've been clinging to."

"Like Corrine and the kids, I've been hoping and praying for years that you'd find peace," Olga replied. "I'm so happy for you, Roger. I'll just keep on supporting all of you. That's what family is all about."

"We can all thank God that Roger's mom came to him in a vision," Corrine added.

"Yes indeed," Roger said shaking his head. "Who would have thought it would take her spirit to get me on track again?"

"You should contact Hartmann and his wife," Corrine continued. "They've been very concerned for you. When you left for Manitoba I sent Hartmann the three letters that your cousin sent you regarding William reporting your family to the SS and then him taking the inheritance. I couldn't remember if you gave him a copy of your grandfather's will so I included a copy of it. He has turned everything over to his lawyer friend."

"Thanks so much for looking out for me when I was so out of it I couldn't look out for myself. You're right. We should phone Hartmann and Elsie. I'll phone them tomorrow."

"So good to hear your voice again," Hartmann began when Roger got him on the phone. "I've been worried sick about you. The last time I talked to Corrine, you were scheduled for shock treatments."

"I had shock treatments. They helped some, but it was my mother's spirit that turned the tide for me. For the first time in my life I'm starting to think straight."

Roger told Hartmann of Corrine's accident, her recovery, the visit of his mother's spirit and all the other remarkable things that had transpired in the last few days.

"I'm overjoyed that Corrine's on the mend and that after all these years you've finally gotten this forgiveness thing straight. Trust Divine Providence for the spirit of your mother to get you back on the right track. It's good that you are moving home again. As soon as my lawyer friend, Alder, learned that Freda had passed on, he began pursuing your grandfather's estate with a vengeance. You see, he, like you, had an axe to grind. Alder is German, but was imprisoned during the war for taking a stand against all the Aryan crap. He's optimistic that something positive will come out of it. As you can imagine, there's not too much sympathy for the Nazi philosophy here in Germany anymore."

"If we have the money, Corrine, the kids and I would like to visit Germany, Poland and the Ukraine this summer. My mother's spirit told me it would help me in this forgiveness thing if I could go back to the spots where my family was killed."

"That's good advice. My wife and I would be happy to drive you and your family around when you come over here this summer. If there's a problem with your finances, just let me know and I can help you out with that too. I'll be retiring in June, so we won't have any time constraints for the summer. It would be wise for you to start getting your family's passports ready for your visits to Poland and the Ukraine. It can take a fair amount of time. Elsie and I will get going here on our passports."

"Thank you for the offer of financial help, Hartmann, but we will only accept help if we really are short and only on the condition that it is a loan. We'll get going on the visa and passport thing right away. You'll never know how much Corrine and I appreciate your support."

"Finding out that you and Corrine are back together and that she's on the mend after her accident is such good news," Elsie added on their extension. "It means so much to us. It's wonderful that you're experiencing the power of forgiveness."

CHAPTER 21

Work at the garage was going well for Roger and he was fitting right in. The kids were thrilled that Papa was home every evening.

"I'm a bit on the tense side," Roger said to Corrine Friday evening of the second week he was home. "I know I should make things right with Erich, but it's going to be hard because I don't really feel like doing it. On second thought, I remember Mama saying you couldn't wait to forgive until you felt like it or you'd never do it. If you don't mind, maybe you could come to the lodge with me early tomorrow morning. You could visit the girls while I see Erich."

By seven the next morning, Roger and Corrine were on their way to the old folks' home. While Corrine visited with the night staff, Roger headed to Erich's office and knocked on his door. Erich looked anything but comfortable when Roger stepped inside.

"I have an apology to make to you," Roger said in German, extending his hand towards Erich. As they shook hands there was a perplexed look on Erich's face. "I had reason for taking you to task for taking advantage of Corrine, but perhaps I got carried away and went too far. I was going through my own personal hell, but that's no excuse. As of two weeks ago, Corrine and I are back together and doing well."

"I'm so happy to hear that," Erich replied. "I accept your apology. I'd also like to apologize for my part in what happened between Corrine and me. My wife and I are getting along much better now too. Thank you for being big enough to come to me. You're a stronger man than I am."

"I'm happy for you and your wife," Roger continued. "Sometimes we have to do a whole lot of living before we start to do some learning. At least that's been my experience. Corrine says she'll be returning to work soon. Hopefully, we can all turn over a new leaf now."

Roger was looking happy as he and Corrine left the lodge.

"A couple of weeks ago if you had told me how liberating this 'forgiving bit' is, I would have laughed at you," Roger said as they walked home. "Thank God my mama set me straight."

Three weeks after starting at Camrose, Roger took over the position as shop foreman. As it was a small garage with just one other mechanic, he still did some repair work.

Soon, Corrine was back working at the lodge.

"We are so blessed as a family," she said to Roger one evening. "A few months back, I was in a coma and you were in a mental institute. Now here we are back together and both of us employed again."

"Yes, we're fortunate all right. Hopefully, we'll have a bit of clear sailing now."

The next week, Corrine got a puzzling letter from Irma Shultz, her old midwife for Rosie's birth. It was the first time Corrine had heard from her since Rosie was born.

Dear Corrine,

I did not know of your whereabouts. It took a lot of sleuthing, but I was finally able to make contact with your mom for your address. My personal news is not that good. I've been battling colon cancer for the last eighteen months and now it has started spreading to my other organs. I'd very much like to see you and your husband before I pass on. There are things I'd like to discuss with you in person. If by chance you would be visiting Germany in the near future I'd ask that you look me up. I'll look forward to your reply.

Sincerely, Irma Shultz

Corrine was perplexed with Irma's letter and wondered why, after all these years, she would need to see them. She wrote back that they'd look her up when they visited Germany in July.

Soon Hartmann, Elsie, Corrine and Roger had all the documents their families would need to visit Poland and the Ukraine. Corrine, Roger, the kids and Olga had their flight to Germany booked for the eleventh of July.

Corrine couldn't have been happier. With Roger home every night, they were a complete family again. Roger had been an excellent soccer player when he attended school in Poland. He began coaching the kids in the game after school and on Saturdays. Without fail, every night before falling asleep, Corrine thanked The Almighty for restoring them as a family.

On the second of July, Conrad phoned Roger late in the evening.

"Sorry to phone so late, but I have bad news. Hans has just passed away. He had a heart attack while he was eating supper. His wife called me and I met them at the hospital. It was a massive heart attack and there was nothing the doctors could do. He passed away about an hour after they got him into emergency. The funeral is next Saturday and the family requested that you be a pallbearer. I'll be out to see you tomorrow morning. There are some business decisions we're going to have to make."

"That is a shock. Did he or anyone else know of his heart condition?"

"From what his wife Edith said, it was a total surprise for everyone, including Hans. Although he was somewhat overweight, he was in good health. According to Edith, a lot of his family died young from heart problems though. Anyway, we'll talk some more in the morning. We'll have to discuss what we do with the Camrose business."

Roger held the phone in his hand for some time, looking quite out of it.

"Bad news?" Corrine asked.

"Horrible news," Roger blurted out. "Hans died of a heart attack. Just after supper I guess. They want me to be a pallbearer. Man, what a shock. Conrad is coming out in the morning to talk over the business end of things. It sounds like it's going to knock everything for a loop."

"That is heavy news," Corrine replied. "I heard some of the conversation. It sounds like no one saw this coming."

"That's what Conrad said. What concerns me is where does this leave us? I thought it was supposed to be clear sailing for us after I got myself straightened out. How the hell will we manage now with a mortgage and car payments if I'm out of work? Why is the universe allowing this to happen to us?"

"Don't you remember the messages from your mom that things would work out for us? We just have to have faith that they will. Instead of worrying about ourselves, maybe we should be concerned for Edith and her family. I can't imagine the pain she's going through."

"Thanks Dear, I needed that," Roger replied after a long pause. "I see how easy it is for me to lapse back into my old sick mindset."

After phoning Edith and giving her their condolences, Roger and Corrine turned in. For the first time in months, Roger had an uneasy sleep. There was none of the groans and screams from the slave labor camp that he used to experience, but in his dreams, he was back in that era.

The next morning, Conrad stopped at the garage. He, Roger and Ernie met in the office.

"The long and short of it is that we're in a real bind," Conrad began. "Hans and I borrowed the money to buy Reinhold out and like real idiots we never put life insurance on the loan. It's a little too early to know how it will all work out, but Edith wasn't all that happy about us buying this business in the first place. The other problem is that I'm the silent partner. I'm a pharmacist, not a mechanic. I'd never be able to run the businesses on a day-to-day basis. Now, if you can manage running the garage here in Camrose, Roger, I think we're going to have to take Ernie back to run our operation in Edmonton. Edith talked to me briefly last night. She said her gut feeling was that in the future we should consider selling both businesses. Both Edith and I feel we shouldn't be too quick in making any business decisions so if we do sell the businesses, it won't be for a while. Edith mentioned that when we sell the Camrose garage, you should be given first grabs and I agree with her. Our purchase price last winter was $90,000."

"Thanks, but where in blazes would Corrine and I come up with that kind of money? We're able to make ends meet, but have no big wad of cash stashed away. On second thought, there might be a glimmer of hope," Roger added after a long pause. "I had an inheritance of some $150,000 from the old country that was swindled from me just before the war ended. I have an accountant friend in Germany who is working on trying to get it back for me, but at this point, we can only look at it as a possibility."

"If I remember correctly, you're going to Europe on holidays fairly soon."

"Yes, we'll be leaving on the eleventh of the month."

"I'll sit down with Edith after the funeral. Hopefully before you take off we can give you a little better idea of what's going to happen. At any rate, by the time you return we should have a handle on what we're going to do with both businesses. Until you get back, things will remain status quo with the Camrose branch."

The day before the funeral, Roger phoned Hartmann regarding Hans's death. He also wanted to see if there was anything new with Jacob's estate.

"First, let me extend my condolences to you and Corrine over the death of your boss," Hartmann said. "Now as to your grandpa's estate, according to my lawyer friend, Alder Pohl, things look fairly promising in that regards. Because of William's strong anti-Jewish track record, his lawyer recognizes they would not do well in court and has requested that just the lawyers meet with a mediator. The decision reached by the mediator would be final. The lawyers are scheduled to meet with the mediator on the fifteenth of July. Alder feels confident the decision will be made in your and your cousin's favor. He said the only thing in question would be the amount awarded you two."

"Does Mr. Pohl have any rough idea what the award might be? What if William says he's spent it all, gave it all to that 'Society for the Elimination of Jews' or claims bankruptcy?"

"Well, I was talking with Alder a few days ago. The total value of Jacob's estate by his reckoning was in the neighborhood of $300,000 at the time of Freda's death. Alder says we don't have to worry about William trying to disregard the mediator's decision. William apparently is walking on eggshells and if he's not careful he could be charged with embezzlement or theft. It's common knowledge that he owns a large construction company and over the years has been doing a lot of work for the government on repairing infrastructure damaged by the war. He does not need poor publicity and apparently he is quite wealthy. Alder's and William's lawyers have individually assembled all the pertinent facts. The mediator has stipulated that other than the three of them, only you, your cousin Harry and William can attend and then only as observers and if necessary, resource people."

"We'll be arriving in Germany on the eleventh. I certainly want to be present at the mediation session if it's at all possible."

"The mediation session is taking place here in Rohn where we live. I'd be happy to pick you up and bring you here. You said you'd be spending a couple of days at your mother-in-law's place as soon as you arrive. Phone me when you get to her place. I can pick you up on the fifteenth. It will only take a few hours to drive from your mother-in-law's place to Rohn. Once we meet, we'll discuss things more."

Hans's funeral was a sad time for Roger and Corrine. However, the news from Hartmann regarding the estate gave them hope that justice would soon be served.

Early on the eleventh, Roger, Corrine, Rosie, Gregory and Olga boarded the airplane and were to their way. Corrine looked down at the patch work of fields, the wooded lands, rivers and lakes.

To the drone of the airplane engines, she whispered, "What lies ahead, Lord? There's still a lot of uncertainty. Help it all work out for us. Thank you for restoring our family."

CHAPTER 22

Helga and Rena were at the airport to greet Corrine, Roger, Olga and the kids.

"You don't know how good it is to see you all again," Helga said to Corrine as she hugged her. "I was so worried for you, Roger and the kids. God alone knows how much I've prayed that your family would be restored. It's so wonderful to see those prayers answered. I'm sorry Gottfried couldn't be here. Right now he's working on a project in Sweden. Hopefully, he'll get back before you have to leave."

"I have so much to be thankful for," Roger responded. "Putting up with me for all these years was a heavy burden on Corrine and the kids. Olga has been a Godsend for our family. I know we couldn't have survived without her. It was my mother's spirit though that finally brought me to my senses."

"Yes, Corrine wrote us about that. It makes us realize that the power of motherhood doesn't end at death."

It had been an exhausting trip so after a late supper, everyone turned in for the night.

"I have such a strong feeling of foreboding that I just can't seem to shake," Corrine whispered to Roger once they were in bed. "It's about Irma Shultz wanting to see us. It's hard to put it in words, but it feels like there's a heavy burden on my soul."

"It's natural to feel a bit uptight not knowing what she needs to talk to us about, but there's nothing we can do right now. We'll just have to leave it in God's hands."

"I guess you're right. It's foolish for me to be wrought up about it. I'll just have to attempt to put my mind at ease and try not to worry."

Despite Corrine's feelings of foreboding, she was soon asleep and awoke refreshed. After breakfast, she phoned Irma's hospital and advised them that Roger and she would be in to see Irma in the afternoon.

Roger phoned Hartmann after Corrine made her call. "We'll be driving over to see Corrine's old mid-wife this morning. She's in very poor health and wrote that she wants to see us. We'll be using Corrine's mother's car. Maybe we can meet at your place before the mediation meeting."

"That would suit us fine. We'll talk then and make plans for our trip to Poland and the Ukraine. Good to hear you again, Roger. Welcome back to Germany."

After breakfast, Roger and Corrine borrowed Helga's car and left to see Irma. Helga and Olga used Gottfried's car to take the kids sightseeing. Despite giving herself a stern lecture, as the miles slipped by, Corrine's apprehension was growing again.

When they arrived at the hospital, Corrine went in to see Irma while Roger stayed in the waiting room. Irma was very aged and as Corrine hugged her she was taken aback at how frail she looked.

"So wonderful to see you again," Irma said, in a very weak voice. "I'm very sick and I have been praying non-stop that you'd get here in time. Where is Roger and did you bring the kids?"

"Roger is in the waiting room. We left the kids with my mother. I didn't know if you'd want to speak just to me, or to all of us."

"It's good you didn't bring the kids today. It would be best for now just to talk to you and Roger. The two of you can decide later whether or not to share with the kids."

"Okay, I'll go get Roger," Corrine replied, looking most apprehensive.

"Good to see you again," Roger said, striding over to Irma's bed and grasping both of her hands.

Irma smiled and continued, "I know I'm not long for this world and felt I had to attend to all the loose ends while I'm still able to. Could you move a bit closer? My voice is weak."

Roger and Corrine moved their chairs closer to the bed and Irma continued.

"I have a confession to make and I hope and pray you'll understand the wherefores and whys of what Doctor Weidman and I did. When you delivered some eleven years ago, Corrine, Hilda delivered just hours before you."

Corrine nodded, looking very perplexed.

"As you'll recall, she was going to give her baby up for adoption and the adoptive parents had already been picked out. Well, three weeks before Hilda delivered; the adoptive mother-to-be became pregnant and advised us that she and her husband were no longer interested in adoption. I shared this information with no one except the doctor. As Hilda had agreed to give her baby up and had signed the necessary papers, I didn't tell her. When she delivered, I assumed the baby would end up in an orphanage until it could be adopted by someone else. Now please try to understand the rationale for what the doctor and I did and try to brace yourselves."

"Your delivery was difficult, Corrine, and you were heavily sedated. You see, your baby was stillborn. The little blond girl was very abnormal. Anyway, we had to move fast. The doctor and I agreed that you were a good responsible couple. The baby I brought in to you after your sedation wore off was Hilda's baby girl. Please forgive the doctor and me for playing God. Doctor Weidman has since passed on, God rest his soul. We made a very quick decision based both on our concern for the baby's welfare and our concern for you two. After all these years, I'm still in a quandary whether I should ask for your forgiveness, your thanks or maybe both."

"Hilda never made any inquiry to me about how the baby was making out with her adoptive parents. A few years after you got Rosie, I ran into Hilda's old employer. She said Hilda had quit working for her a few months after her baby was born and the last she'd heard, immigrated to Argentina. If you think Rosie would be up to handling this information, I'd love to see her."

Tears were slipping down Irma's cheeks. She reached over, took Corrine's hand and whispered, "Please forgive me if you can."

Corrine and Roger sat in stunned silence, trying desperately to absorb the shocking news.

"You did what you thought was right," Roger finally responded, shaking his head. "Without question, I'm so shocked that I can't think and by the look in Corrine's face I'd say she's even more shocked than I am."

"Roger's right," Corrine interjected between sobs. "I can't say if I can forgive you right now. You'll have to give me time to get all of this through my head. We'll stop in to see you tomorrow."

Sobbing uncontrollably, Corrine jumped to her feet and headed for the door. Roger patted Irma's hand and followed.

"I just can't take it," Corrine wailed. "It's so unbelievable, finding out that Rosie's not our daughter. Why is this happening to us? How will our darling girl be able to handle this terrible news?"

"Before you come right apart, remember Rosie is still our daughter. Instead of worrying yourself sick about Rosie's reaction, maybe we should come right out and tell her."

"How, oh how, does the universe expect me to forgive that woman for what she's done?" Corrine cried, "never, never, never!"

"Maybe you should remember the story of a man you know who spent most of his life shouting those same words. Ask yourself if there's a possibility that what Irma and the doctor did was in God's overall plan for Rosie and us."

"I don't know. I'm just so shocked I don't know what to think. Really, all Irma had to do was to tell us our baby had died and asked us to adopt the other little girl."

"And can you say without question that considering the pain we'd have felt over having just lost our daughter and the coolness Hilda exhibited towards you that we'd have ended up with Rosie? We just have no way of knowing the answer to that."

"I don't know. Maybe you're right. Do you think we could stay in a hotel overnight? I've got to get my thinking straight before I meet with Irma again or for that matter tell Rosie and Gregory."

It was approaching six, so after phoning Corrine's mom and Olga that they'd be spending the night, Roger and Corrine booked into a hotel. After having supper at a café, they headed back to their hotel room.

"For me, the biggest thing is that despite Irma's and the doctor's good intentions, for all these years I feel we've been played as suckers," Corrine said when they got to their room. "You see, we've also been robbed of grieving for our dead baby. On second thought, of far more importance is how Rosie will handle the news or for that matter Gregory."

"Maybe if we look at the big picture, Irma and the doctor really did the right thing," Roger replied putting his arm around Corrine. "There's no question it's shocking though. As for Rosie I wouldn't sell her short. We have to remember she was very supportive of you when you told her of your affair with Erich."

"That's true, I guess. I wonder when we should we tell her and Gregory?"

"I think the sooner we tell them the better. I'd suggest tomorrow."

"In regards to holding a grudge against Irma for what she did, remember what that did to my life."

"I see your point. If you don't mind now, let me think on it myself for a spell."

Corrine and Roger spent the rest of the evening individually trying to work their way through this new maze. Finally, they turned in. Although Roger had come to peace with the new development and was soon asleep, Corrine spent many hours tossing and turning. She vacillated between feeling numb, feeling guardedly positive, to feeling betrayed. Overriding these emotions was the fear of how Rosie and Gregory would react to the startling news. After hours of agonizing, Corrine fell into a troubled sleep.

Suddenly, she was back walking on the path beside the river she and Roger often walked in their courting days. It was a most vivid dream. A lady was walking beside her. As her companion was wearing a hooded jacket, Corrine could not see her face.

"You are going through a hard time coming to grips with this startling news about your two daughters," the lady began. "With your first pregnancy, had your baby lived, she'd have been in a vegetative state. The universe had other plans. They realized the baby born of the young girl Hilda would have a very hard life. You recall your dream shortly after you had the baby?"

"Yes the dream is coming back to me now. I see what was meant by the baby changing from a light complexioned little girl to a dark one. I remember now that when I was having the dream I couldn't make heads or tails of it and by the time I awoke I'd forgotten most of it."

"You're beginning to understand it now. This may be hard for you to grasp, but the soul that had been in your sister Rosie decided to come back into your baby daughter's body. Before you gave birth, God was aware that your baby was malformed and would not live. The Creator also knew that Hilda's baby would become yours and Roger's daughter. To that end, before Hilda gave birth, your sister's soul was placed in her baby. It was the Creator's decision and we should not question the powers that be. I trust this explanation will help you through this heavy time. You need not worry about Rosie's or Gregory's reaction. Like with you and Roger, it will shock them, but they'll understand and accept it."

"Thank you so much," Corrine replied. "You don't know how much your explanation has already helped me."

The lady softly placed her hand on Corrine's shoulder, turned towards her, smiled and disappeared.

"Oh my God!" Corrine exclaimed, sitting up in bed. "That was Maria, Roger's mother."

"You called me?" Roger muttered still half asleep.

"I just had the most wonderful dream. I'm positive your mother's spirit came to me and explained everything about our baby's death and us getting Rosie."

"It's all falling into place," Roger said after Corrine finished telling him about her dream.

"That's right," Corrine added. "Now I'm remembering the dream I had years ago when I could see the baby in my womb changing from a blond baby to a dark haired baby. As you say it's all making sense now."

"I guess Mama is at it again. Her message is so unreal that it makes sense. It almost blows the mind though. It sounds like it's helped you."

"Yes, it's helped me an awful lot. I feel like a heavy load has been taken off my back. I think we should go tell the kids this morning and then maybe bring them back with us to see Irma in the afternoon."

"I'm with you on that, but let's try to get a bit more sleep. It's just 3 AM."

They got an early start and by ten they were back at Helga's place.

There were scads of leftovers from the previous day's meals and in jig time the ladies had a picnic lunch ready. By eleven, Roger, Corrine, Rosie and Gregory were back on the road to see Irma again. At twelve, they pulled off at a roadside picnic table.

"I have some very strange news for you, Rosie and Gregory," Corrine began hesitantly. "I've been praying all morning that you'll be able to accept it. Yesterday we found out from my old midwife that you, Rosie, are not our biological child."

Corrine went on, filling the kids in on what biological meant, what they had learned from Irma the previous afternoon and ending up describing the dream she had.

"I'm trying hard to forgive Irma for what she did, but it's difficult."

"It is sort of shocking," Rosie replied hesitantly, "but you must forgive her, Mom. Remember what Grandma Maria told Papa, 'we must forgive to live.' And remember, last night in your dream Grandma Maria said it was all in God's plan."

"You're such a wise, kind girl," Corrine said. There were tears in her eyes as she hugged both Rosie and Gregory.

"What about you Gregory? How do you feel about all of this?"

"I don't care about this bylogy thing," he replied with real fervor. "Rosie's still my sister. Can I have another piece of chicken?"

"Are you sure you're okay with all of this, Rosie?" Corrine continued.

"Yes, I am, Mom. You and Papa are my real parents and besides, like Grandma said, it was what God wanted to do and so He let it happen."

Soon they were on the road again, heading for the hospital.

"Kids are so much wiser than we give them credit for," Corrine mused, shaking her head; "so much wiser."

When they reached the hospital, Corrine went in to see Irma while Roger and the kids stayed in the waiting room.

"It's been a heavy time for Roger and me," Corrine began, sitting close to Irma's bed and taking her hand. "I wanted to spend a few minutes with you alone and then I'll go get Roger and the kids. They're in the waiting room."

"When I left yesterday, I was in so much shock I couldn't think straight. After thinking on it for several hours with Roger's help and after a mind-bending dream, I've finally found peace. You mentioned something yesterday that says it all. You said that after all these years you still didn't know whether you should ask for forgiveness, thanks or both. Well I accept your request for forgiveness and I offer you my thanks."

As Corrine told Irma of her dream and then the kid's reactions, tears of relief ran down the old lady's face.

"God is so wise and good," she finally whispered. "You'll never know what that dream means to me too. For all these years I wondered whether Doctor Weidman and I went too far. This dream gives me the assurance that what we did was really in the Universe's plan."

"Yesterday afternoon I couldn't say that, but yes, I now believe what you and Doctor Weidman did was God working through you. I'll go and get Roger and the kids now."

When they were all in Irma's room, Rosie walked over to the bed and took Irma's hand.

"Mom told me all of what happened," Rosie began hesitantly. "I want you to know I'm not mad at you or upset. It is a little scary though, but like my grandma in the dream said, it was what God wanted to do."

"Thank you so much, Rosie. You're a very mature, kind, young lady. I'm sure your mom and dad are proud of you."

"Thanks," Rosie whispered.

"The doctor and I had your baby buried in the Pleasant View Cemetery here in the city," Irma continued, turning to Roger and Corrine. "The grave is marked. As you'll recall, Rosie was registered as your daughter and it's probably best to leave it that way. All the information on the biological parents is with Doctor Weidman's widow. She dropped by to visit me a few weeks ago. You see, at Rosie's birth, Doctor Weidman and I put all the information we had on Hilda and the little we were able to get on her boyfriend on your file. I didn't tell Mrs. Weidman why, but advised her of the possibility that you might need this information. I don't think Mrs. Weidman was ever aware of what her husband and I did. She said she'd be happy to make that information available to you if you requested it."

"We should be leaving now," Corrine said. "We don't want to tire you too much. Before we head for home we'll drop in on you again."

"Thank you all so much for your visit," Irma concluded. "I'm now at peace for the first time in many years. I'll be looking forward to your next visit."

Once they left the hospital, Corrine phoned the Weidman's, talked to the maid and made arrangements to pick up the information.

Corrine and Roger picked up the envelope without incident and on the kid's insistence stopped at a café for ice cream sundaes.

"Would you like to see our little girl's grave?" Roger asked Corrine once they were in the car again.

"I'd really like that. What do you think, kids?"

"Sure, that would be okay," Rosie replied. "I'd kind of like to see where my little sister is buried."

Gregory looked up from his comic book and nodded his approval.

It had been many years since Roger and Corrine lived in Demzig, but they found the cemetery without too much difficulty.

"Holy mackerel," Gregory exclaimed when he first saw all the grave stones. "There must be millions of dead people. Where do they all come from?"

It was without question a huge graveyard. An old gentleman who was cemetery guide led them to a small wooden cross and then took his leave.

With tears in her eyes, Corrine bent over and read the faded words on the cross.

Baby Goodz Stillborn May 1 1948
May Your Tiny Being Rest in Peace

"I'm feeling sort of sad," Rosie said, deep in thought, "but there is one thing I don't understand, Papa. In Mom's dream, Grandma said that the soul that was to go into this little baby went into me. Didn't this little baby have a soul then?"

"There are things in this world that God says we don't need an answer for," Roger replied, wiping the tears from his eyes. "There was my mama's spirit visiting me a few months ago. Then there's Mom. She sometimes is able to see into the future, or see spirits. We don't know how these things happen, but they do. When I can't understand certain things, I just say, 'the answer is blowing in the wind.'"

"That means we might never know the answer, right Papa?"

"That's right Rosie. In this life we'll never know the answer."

"I was wondering if we should put up a small grave stone," Corrine said as they were walking back to the car. "That little cross is pretty weathered."

"Yes, that's a good idea," Roger replied. "If my inheritance comes through, we'll have the money to do it before we leave. If we don't get the money we'll have to wait until we get home and can put together a few extra dollars. Those tombstones are fairly expensive."

"I'm so glad we came," Rosie said turning around and gazing back at the cemetery. "Sometimes I wonder if I'm in a movie. It's all been so scary and sad, but now I know my little sister is with God."

CHAPTER 23

Early Friday morning, Hartmann and Elsie drove to Helga's place to pick up Roger and Corrine. After coffee, Hartmann, Elsie, Roger and Corrine were on the way to Rohn for the hearing.

"You look like you're under a bit of pressure, Roger," Hartmann said as they were driving along. "I imagine you're apprehensive about the hearing."

"Yes, it does put me a bit on edge and then we've had some very strange news about Rosie that Corrine and I are still trying to cope with."

Corrine and Roger told Hartmann and Elsie the news from Irma that Rosie was not their biological child and the dream Corrine had.

"You're family has come through a lot," Elsie responded. "Our heart goes out to all of you. What a shock that must have been. The way all of you are managing it is a sign of the real depth and strength of your family."

"I concur with Rosie that it was all in God's plan, Hartmann added. "Just imagine how you would have handled this news, Roger, if it had happened before you got yourself straightened out."

"Yes, you're right," Roger replied. "I'm sure there was no way I could have managed it a few months back."

"A couple of nights ago I was the one who was having real trouble with the whole thing," Corrine interjected. "It was Roger who was the strong one this time. He helped me immeasurably."

"There is something else that's gnawing away at me," Roger added. "When my mother's spirit visited me she said there was a mystery about William that I'd learn about in time. I guess we'll just have to wait on that one."

After dinner they drove to the courthouse. Hartmann introduced them to Alder Pohl, his lawyer friend. Following introductions, Hartmann accompanied Corrine and Elsie to a nearby department store so the ladies could shop. Alder and Roger went to the mediation room and met with Ernest Knob, the mediator and Richard Shrek, William's lawyer.

"William and Roger's cousin Harry have elected not to come," Ernest began. "Roger, no doubt your lawyer has explained that you're here as an observer and resource person. I may, if necessary, ask you for clarification on some issues."

"All of Jacob's estate was transferred from Poland to Germany before the Russian occupation of Poland," Ernest continued. "Other than his will which is honored by both countries, the handling of the estate is now all under German law. Both briefs accept that William was given the power of attorney over Freda as she was deemed mentally incapable of handling her own affairs. Any transactions made by William on Freda's behalf before her death were legal. As stated in Jacob's will, his estate was to be used exclusively for Freda's welfare and the balance to be given Jacob's two grandsons on Freda's death."

"I have documentation from the matron of the lodge where Freda stayed that William did not visit or have anything to do with his sister after arranging to have her hospitalized with the exception of sending her a number of most repugnant racial letters. He did not advance her any money while she was hospitalized, nor did he pay for Freda's funeral or even attend it."

"My client advised me he made a number of visits and phone calls to the hospital checking on his sister," Richard responded.

"If William did make contact with his sister, you did not include any proof of those contacts in your brief," the mediator continued. "All phone calls and visits to a patient are recorded. According to the matron there were none from William."

The mediator handed copies of the matron's letter to the two lawyers.

"The letters William sent his sister are damning for your client," Ernest added, turning to Richard. "Here are copies of those letters which are signed either by your client or an SS officer. Alder provided me these letters in his brief. I'll give you a few minutes to read them. I have the original copies, so you may keep them."

As Richard was reading the letters he was constantly shaking his head. Without making comment, he placed the letters in his briefcase.

"What we've covered up until now is academic," Ernest said, handing both lawyers copies of Jacob's will. "Now Richard; if you have documentation showing that William used a portion of Jacob's estate to benefit Freda when she was incapacitated, then that portion would be deducted from the estate. I see no such documentation in your brief."

"I have no documentation to that effect," Richard replied.

Ernest nodded.

"Had this matter ended up in court, Richard, your client could have faced criminal charges. In civil court there is no question in my mind that in addition to paying back the estate, there probably would have been additional costs for mental anguish."

"In his brief, Alder asks only for the total value of the estate plus interest incurred since Freda's death for his clients. I am convinced that this is a fair request. My decision, then, is that the value of the estate at Freda's death plus incurred interest be paid the two grandsons, Roger and Harry. By my calculations, the estate was valued at 305,000 American dollars at Freda's death. With incurred interest of $23,000, this makes a total settlement of $328,000 American for the two claimants. That would be $164,000 American dollars each for Roger and Harry."

"Alder and I agreed that on behalf of the claimants that your decision would be final," Richard replied. In conversation with my client this morning, he stated that should your decision award the two claimants a settlement, he'd request two years to pay that settlement out."

"I hardly think so," Ernest countered. "He's withheld the funds that were rightfully Roger's and Harry's for a number of years. In addition, the costs for my services will be borne by your client. That's my decision. Now if we could adjourn for an hour, with the help of the court secretary, I'll put all this in writing."

"I understand," Richard said, smiling. "William has provided me with two signed checks for the two claimants. I just have to fill in the amount. I'll have them filled out and certified by the time we reconvene."

After getting the two checks certified, Richard rejoined Roger and Alder. When they returned to the mediator's office,

Ernest had copies of his decision for Roger and the lawyers. Richard in turn handed over the two certified checks to the mediator. Ernest glanced at the checks to see if the amounts were right and then handed the two checks to Alder.

As they were leaving, Roger excused himself from Alder and caught up with Richard.

"I'd like you to give this note to William," Roger began. "As you're his legal representative, feel free to read it."

Richard opened the folded note and silently read:

William: Today justice has been finally served for my cousin Harry and me. I forgive you for all the pain you have inflicted on your sister Freda, my mother Maria, my grandpa Jacob and me. I alone am alive so I speak for them. We hold no malice toward you.

Roger

"That's very commendable of you, Roger," Richard said after a long pause. "You are wise to rid yourself of hatred and anger. In my practice I know of many who harbor hatred and it gets them nowhere. Unfortunately, William is one of those. He's financially successful, but is a very despondent man. His wife left him years ago because of his mean-spirited ways. Wealth cannot buy happiness. I'll make sure he gets the note."

"Thank you so much for all your hard work," Roger said when he caught up with Alder. "Is there any way you'd allow me to pay you?"

"You already have. That look of happiness on your face when I handed you the check is payment enough. At this time in my life, I'm not in need of money. You see, I had a vested interest in seeing justice implemented in this case. As you may have heard from Hartmann, although I am German, I was imprisoned during the war for my stand against the racial policies of the Nazis. Today is as much my day as it is yours."

At five o'clock, Alder and Roger met with Hartmann, Elsie and Corrine.

"Again, thanks so much for your help, Alder," Roger said. "If you won't accept anything for all your services at least allow my wife and I to take you, Hartman and Elsie out for supper."

"Well, okay, I guess I could agree to that."

"By the look on both your faces I'd say things went well," Hartmann interjected.

Roger was so overcome with emotion he could not reply. Silently he handed Hartmann the written decision of the mediator and the two certified checks.

"Good show!" Hartmann exclaimed. After reading the decision he handed it and the checks to Corrine.

"What a day!" Corrine cried out exuberantly. "It's hard to believe Roger and Harry were each awarded $164,000. Alder and Hartmann, thank you for all your help."

As they were eating supper, Roger mentioned the note he'd written William.

"That's most admirable of you Roger," Alder responded. "There was some interesting information I uncovered about William when I was preparing my case that I kept to myself. After hearing about your note, I now feel I can share this news with you. I do not know if you knew this, or if Freda or William even knew it, but William was Freda's half-brother. Freda's biological mother died giving birth to her. Freda's father remarried less than a year later. William was born two years after his father remarried. William was apparently an officer in the army when he began researching his parent's ancestry. He learned that there was Jewish blood on his maternal grandmother's side. Most of us would think nothing of this, but, after discovering this, William became fixated on his anti-Jewish stance. I guess that proves that anyone can be an idiot regardless of one's racial extraction or parts thereof."

Shaking his head, Roger replied. "Thank God I got my head straightened enough to handle that information."

After supper, Hartmann drove Alder back to his car and then they headed to Hartmann's and Elsie's place.

"What are your immediate plans?" Hartmann asked. "And when do we go to Poland and the Ukraine?"

"Well, tomorrow I think we should look after Harry's check. I think I'll wire most of my money to my bank in Camrose. After that we could leave for Poland anytime."

"I can give you a hand transferring the money," Hartmann said. "What say for tonight we head to our place and punish a couple or three bottles of wine?"

"I'm for that," Corrine interjected. "I think we've all earned a drink or two."

"You don't know how relieved I am," Roger said. "The money is important all right, but of equal importance is that justice has finally been served and that Grandpa's and Freda's wishes have been honored."

"It's nothing short of a miracle how things have made such a turn-around for your family," Hartmann said.

"You're so right," Corrine responded. "Last year Roger was getting shock treatments and I was in a coma."

"Corrine and I are so grateful for all your support," Roger added.

"We didn't want to mention this until after the mediation hearing, but Hartmann and I are making plans to immigrate to Canada," Elsie said as they were pulling up their driveway. "As you know, Hartmann lost his first wife, daughter and mother to the war and his dad has passed away. I have two children from my first marriage, but they left Germany some time ago. My son Richard is an engineer and he immigrated to California three years ago. My daughter, Rose and her husband immigrated to Toronto last year. With both Hartmann's and my parents gone, we have no close family keeping us here."

"About two months ago we got word from Elsie's daughter that their family is going to be relocating in Edmonton," Hartmann continued. "As we don't have much keeping us in this country anymore, last week we took the plunge and made out our application to immigrate. It's our plan to locate in the Edmonton area."

"Wow! We'll be close neighbors then," Corrine added. "What wonderful news!"

Soon they were at Hartmann's and Elsie's place. Over a few bottles of wine their discussion continued.

"I understand you'll be buying the Camrose garage as soon as you get back," Hartmann said to Roger.

"That's right. Just before we left on holidays, they set the price at $87,000 for a quick sale. I was given first chance at buying it. Of course the plan to buy it was only possible if I was awarded my inheritance. I'll phone Conrad tomorrow. The original plans were to add another two mechanic bays and a show-room. Before Hans died he was having talks with Volkswagen to put a dealership in Camrose."

"Would you consider making those renovations now and what about going after the dealership?"

"Corrine and I talked about what we should do if we got the inheritance. We both agreed we should buy the garage and possibly try to do the expansion. As for going after the Volkswagen dealership, that's sort of a grey area for us."

"Elsie and I have been talking about your business venture, if you got your inheritance. Now the last thing in the world we want to do is horn in on your plans, but we do have a bit of extra money."

"Well, would you and Elsie be interested in buying into the business?"

"It is a consideration, but would you and Corrine want us in? Be honest with us now, it's your business venture."

"You won't believe this," Corrine replied, "but Roger and I were talking about how good it would be to get you guys into the business. We thought it was just wishful thinking though. We had no idea that immigration was something you were considering."

"It's amazing how we were all thinking on the same page," Hartmann continued. "If you want us to be silent investors, then that would be okay. On the other hand, I'd be interested in helping with the bookkeeping, if you'd want that. I'm finding retirement a bit of a drag and wouldn't mind a bit of productive activity. My English certainly isn't perfect, but I get by."

"My English still leaves a lot to be desired too," Roger said, pouring himself another large glass of wine. "I guess we can all learn. There is a large German community in the Camrose area and I've found a lot of our customers are fairly fluent in German."

"Tomorrow, after we look after handling the money, maybe we should put our ideas down on paper," Hartmann added, topping up his glass. "Tonight, let's celebrate."

The party went on until the wee hours of the morning. Finally, everyone called it a day and turned in.

"What a day it's been," Corrine said once they were in bed. "Are you as excited as I am about this whole business venture?"

"It sounds great to me. I know we can trust Hartmann and Elsie. Hartmann's always been there for us. Being an accountant, he'll have a good handle on the business end of things."

"Remember the note I wrote William? Well, Richard will be delivering it to him. It's strange, but just like forgiving Erich, as soon as I wrote the letter I felt unbelievable relief."

"Good for you. How are you feeling about visiting the death places of your family back in Poland and the Ukraine?"

"I'm not looking forward to it all that much, but I know I have to do it. The first thing I'm going to do when we get back home is see a psychologist. I think I've made good progress, but no doubt they can help me more. I never want to go back into that hellhole of anger and hate."

CHAPTER 24

Everyone slept in and after a late breakfast, Hartmann and Roger went to a bank to open up an account for Harry and deposit his check. They transferred most of Roger's settlement to his Camrose bank account.

In the afternoon Roger phoned Conrad in Edmonton. "Good to hear from you, Roger. How did you make out with your inheritance?"

"Well, we won. My cousin and I got all of our granddad's estate. The decision was made yesterday and my money has been transferred to my Camrose account. Is the deal on the Camrose garage still open for Corrine and me?"

"It sure is, Roger. I'm elated for you and Corrine. Whenever you get back, we can arrange the paper work. I'll phone the garage in Camrose. They were keeping their fingers crossed that you'd be able to swing the deal. We may also have a sale for the Edmonton garage. Ernie and a friend are planning on buying it. Things are clicking into place. We'll talk more when you get back home."

As soon as they got back from the bank, Hartmann and Roger worked on a business proposal. After drawing up a rough draft, they brought Corrine and Elsie in to discuss it in depth.

"Corrine and I will buy the garage for $87,000 as soon as we get back," Roger began. "Hartman figures he and Elsie could finance the expansion up to $75,000. I'll do the day by day operation of the garage while Hartmann will do the books and help in any business decisions."

"I've told Roger that I want him and Corrine to be the principals, while Elsie and I will buy in on a share of the business," Hartmann added. "Our accounting firm did work for one of the directors of Volkswagen so we might have an inside track in getting a dealership for Camrose."

"I think it's a wonderful plan," Elsie said. "Although I love him dearly, it will be good to get Hartmann out of the house again. It can be a real pain with him underfoot all day."

"I'm so happy things are working out so smoothly," Corrine added. "When do you think you'll be coming to Canada?"

"Alder is helping us with the paperwork," Hartmann responded. "He says we should have everything tied up and be able to leave in two months. We should draw up a legal partnership contract now. Elsie and I can then deposit money in a bank in Camrose. This will allow us to start on the expansion as soon as you two get back."

By five that evening, with the help of Alder, they drew up the contract and had it notarized. After an early supper they were on the way to pick up Gregory and Rosie.

The kids, Olga and Helga were ecstatic with the news that Roger got his estate back. The two ladies insisted they have coffee. After a short visit they were on the road again, arriving back quite late at Hartmann's and Elsie's.

In the morning they were on their way to Poland and the Ukraine. Hartmann chose a less travelled scenic route so the kids could get a better view of the rural countryside. In mid-afternoon, they stopped at the site of the old Tank factory. The complex had been changed to a heavy equipment manufacturing plant.

When they stopped for supper they were getting close to the Polish border. The kids were suffering from cabin fever so they decided to call it a day and get an early start in the morning.

The morning dawned windy, cool and overcast. They made it through the border crossing without incident and many hours later were nearing the site of the old slave labor metal demolition plant where Jacob and Roger were interred. After a few dead-ends, they found the location. Most of the old buildings had been demolished and part of the site was now used as a railroad repair yard.

As they drove over the old railroad crossing, Roger was growing very tense. Ahead, to the right he noticed the huge oak tree that stood close to the entrance of their sleeping quarters. Flashes of his stay at the horrific camp played across his mind's eye.

"God, it was awful," he muttered, as Hartmann pulled into a parking area. Roger got out and started walking towards the tree.

An old guard in a tattered uniform slowly shuffled towards him.

"We have come to have a look at the old slave labor recycling work camp," Roger began in Polish. "I worked here during the war."

"You were lucky to have survived," the old man replied, taking a long drag on his roll-your-own cigarette. "My two uncles worked here and they didn't. Those damned Nazis."

"They took me to a tank factory in Germany later in the war," Roger continued. "It was a lot better there."

"Anything would have been better than this place. I was underground for most of the war. It's not perfect now with Russian rule, but a hell of a lot better than when the Nazis ran things. Up ahead you'll see a fence. It's okay to look at everything on this side of the fence, but you're not supposed to cross the fence or take pictures on the other side. Most of the demolition yard was on this side anyway. Just the eating place and the officer and guard quarters were on the other side. We repair all the railroad rolling stock here. Next year they're supposed to expand over on this side. Mind you, they've been saying that for the last three or four years."

After another long pull on his cigarette, the old guard raised his hand in a sort of wave-salute, turned and ambled back to his guard shack.

"If you don't mind, I'll just get Corrine to come with me," Roger said when he returned to the car. "There are some pretty raw memories here."

"Go ahead," Hartmann replied. "Elsie, the kids and I will go back to that little park that's just a few hundred meters back. I don't relish the idea of doing any sight-seeing at this particular spot. My memories of this place aren't that good either. When you're finished, you can join us."

"Over there, just past that big tree was where our sleeping places were," Roger said, walking hand-in-hand with Corrine. "There were four more sleeping quarters to the right of our place, almost up to the fence. Often, there would be bodies outside in front waiting to be hauled away. They were guys who had died in the night. The eating mess and quarters for the guards and officers were on the other side of the fence where the big shed is now. To the left of the tree some hundred meters is where we worked and then left of that the railroad tracks."

As they walked along in silence, Roger tried to orient himself.

Finally, he stopped. "This is about the spot where it happened," he said quietly, a surge of emotion playing across his face.

"This is where Eli, the guard and the soldier died," he added.

Dropping to his knees he glanced upward and whispered, "To those who caused me pain, I forgive."

When Roger stood up his face was relaxed. Wrapping his arms around Corrine he continued, "Mama was right. It's hard to believe, but the weight is lifting."

"I'm so happy for you. You've carried this burden for so many years. You told me that Jacob was murdered here too."

Roger made no reply. He led Corrine farther in. For several minutes he scanned the area south of the fence, trying to get his bearings.

"Grandpa was killed somewhere in this area. It's a little hard to pinpoint the spot as most of the buildings have been removed. Using that big oak tree as my guide point though, I've got it narrowed down to a spot about 50 meters to the west by about 30 meters to the north of where we're standing. Let's walk a grid pattern on this area. We can walk beside each other, say a meter apart."

"You see, Jacob always carried a small silver Star of David in his pocket. The night he was killed I took the Star of David from his pants pocket before they removed his body. That evening, Hartmann went back with me to where Grandpa was killed. I dug a small hole at the murder site. We put the Star of David in the hole and placed a rock on top of it. I only left about an inch of the rock sticking out of the ground. I didn't want it to look too noticeable."

"Do you think there's any chance we'll find it? We have to remember that was more than fifteen years ago and the grass is so tall."

"I'm not sure, but it doesn't look like the ground has been worked up since then. It was off the pathway some 10 meters or so. I'd really like to find it. With the grass being so high, it won't be hard for us to keep on track."

Slowly they walked the pattern, trying to cover every square meter of the plot.

"I'm afraid it's a lost cause," Roger said, disheartened, after they finished walking the grid. "It was probably too much to expect to find it after all these years."

"Let's make a few more passes before we call it quits," Corrine said. "I'll walk here. You walk on the other side."

They started moving again through the tall grass. Corrine had only gone ten meters when she caught something with her toe.

"I might have something here," she called out. "I think it's a rock."

Roger came running over and squatted down. "Maybe this is it. It's about the same size of rock Hartmann and I used."

In a frenzy, Roger began digging the earth away from the rock with his jackknife. Getting the rock loose, he flipped it out of the ground.

"Oh my God," he whispered. "There it is, Grandpa's Star of David."

"My dido, my dido," he sobbed, dropping to his knees. "God rest your soul."

"I forgive," he said softly, glancing upward. "I forgive you, Helmut, for taking my dido's life."

As Roger got to his feet the wind instantly ceased. The cloud cover broke and they were bathed in sunlight. As suddenly as the clouds parted they again covered the sun and the wind started blowing again.

"The universe is pleased with you for forgiving," Corrine said. "That brief bit of sunshine was your sign."

"It's so unreal," Roger replied. "Every time I forgive, my soul feels lighter."

"What do you want to do with this Star of David?" Corrine asked, handing it back to Roger.

"I wonder. Do you think we should bury it under the rock again?"

"I don't think so. It's one of the few keepsakes you have of your grandpa. You should keep it."

"Maybe you're right, but we should put something back under the rock to record that Grandpa died here. I'm sure he has no grave."

On a small piece of paper, Roger wrote:

Jacob Isaac
God Rest your Soul, Grandpa

Corrine had a small metal powder case in her purse. They cleaned out the powder cake and placed the piece of paper inside it. Roger put the case in the hole, placed the rock on top of it and carefully back-filled around the rock.

"Could you sing Grandpa a song, Dear?" Roger whispered. "You have such a beautiful voice."

As they stood hand in hand, Corrine softly sang 'God Be with You Till We Meet Again.' The whispering wind in the tall grass accompanied her bell-like voice. Roger joined in on the chorus.

Still holding hands, Corrine and Roger slowly walked back to the park.

"You've both experienced something very moving," Elsie said, glancing at their faces.

"Yes, we found where both my friend Eli and Grandpa Jacob were killed," Roger answered. "I've made peace with the murderers. What a relief. Do you remember this, Hartmann?" Roger handed him the Star of David.

Hartmann examined it for some time.

"I can't believe it," he finally blurted out. "Can this be the Star of David we buried under that rock to mark the spot where your grandpa died?"

Roger nodded.

"Was it still buried under that rock?"

"Yes, it was still under the rock."

Roger explained the significance of the 'Star of David' to Elsie and the kids.

"What horrible, horrible days they were," Roger added shaking his head.

"Yes, they were sad, awful days," Hartmann continued quietly. "Back then, you were a very angry young man, Roger. I wondered if you'd ever find the power of forgiveness and of greater importance, the peace that forgiveness brings. It's taken many years, but thank God you finally did."

CHAPTER 25

By early evening they were on the road to Jacob's old store. The store had been torn down and replaced by an apartment.

"Lots of memories here," Roger said quietly, a far-away look coming into his eyes. "There are lots of good ones and some not so good ones."

Roger got Hartmann to drive them to the school he had attended. The old two-story brick building was as it had been. The only noticeable change in the school grounds was that the trees looked a bit bigger.

"Lots more memories here," Roger said as they walked about the grounds. "Why can't one turn back life's time clock? I was about eleven when I started to become very angry with life. All those wasted years spent being so hateful and tore up with the Universe."

Roger's cousin Harry and his wife Anne were expecting the group for supper so after visiting the school, they headed out of town to their small farm. As they drove to the farm, Roger gave them a running commentary of farmers Jacob and he bought produce from. A few of the small farms had now been consolidated into large collective ones.

When they arrived at Harry's and Anne's place, Roger translated for Corrine, Hartmann, Elsie and the kids.

"I hope you got the telegram that we were coming," Roger said. "I sent it before we met with the mediator."

"Yes, we got it," Harry replied. "You mentioned the two lawyers were to meet with a mediator and that it looked good for us to get something from Grandpa's estate. How did it go?"

"It went well. You and I each got $164,000 in American dollars. Hartmann here is an accountant. He helped with all of it and we deposited your money in a bank in Germany."

Roger handed Harry his new bank book.

Harry took the bank book, glanced at the figures and then covered his face with his hands. "Praise God," he finally blurted out. "Praise the Almighty. It's been such a long time coming. To be honest with you I got to the place where I was sure we'd never see a cent of Grandpa's estate. After all these years, it's so moving to see some justice for us Jews."

"It is indeed," Roger continued. "How it all came about is a long, long story. You see, Hartmann was a lieutenant in the German army. He was wounded in action in the war and was acting as guard in the slave labor camp that Grandpa and I were in. We became friends. Without question, Hartmann saved my life and got me transferred to the tank factory in Germany."

"Hartmann is an accountant and after Freda died, he and his lawyer friend, Alder, began working on your and my behalf to get the estate straightened out. Both Hartmann and Alder have refused to take payment. Alder said seeing justice served for us and William being put in his place was payment enough for him."

"Thank you," Harry replied. "Anne and I will be forever grateful to those who helped us."

"What wonderful news," Anne said. "With this money maybe we can build a better house."

"I'm with Anne on that," Harry added. "Now that our finances are looked after we might rent our farm out and retire."

"I can help you access your money," Hartmann began with Roger translating. "All we need is the name of your bank and the number of your bank account. We'll be leaving tomorrow for the Ukraine, but will be back this way in a few days. We can drop in again and give you a hand."

"Thank you so much," Harry replied. "This will give Anne and me the time we need to make some plans. There's the temptation to try to sneak out of the country, but with a new house, we'll be comfortable and then, all our family and friends are here."

Anne was preparing a feast while they were visiting and insisted that everyone eat until they were ready to burst. After an evening of sharing memories, it was time to go.

"We'll drop in again the day after tomorrow and help with the money thing," Roger said as they headed out the door.

"Thank you so much," Harry replied. "Here is a small box of some of Freda's stuff we took from her room when she passed on. A few of the things are hers, a few Jacob's."

Roger booked them rooms in the village inn. After breakfast they were on their way. They finally located the spot where Roger's mother had been interned as a slave laborer, but the old factory had been replaced by a housing complex.

When they got to the border crossing east of Kozmin a very officious young Russian guard handled their paper work. Even though the reason for their visit was clearly written on their visiting permit, he asked, "Reason for visit?" in broken Polish.

"We're here to visit the graves of my sister and Dad in Novich," Roger replied. "They, like millions of others, died in Stalin's man-made famine in 1933."

"There never were millions who died in that so-called famine," the guard replied with feeling.

Roger's blood pressure went up noticeably. He was just going to reply when an older guard who had overheard the conversation came strolling over.

"Staz, you're still wet behind the ears. I don't know what they teach you young fellows in Russia these days. There was an awful man-made famine and yes, millions starved. My mother was one of them."

The young guard growled something in Russian and made a hasty retreat.

"Going to Novich I see," the older guard continued. "That area was hard hit."

"It sure was," Roger said. "From what I've heard, over half our village starved. Is there still that crossing about three or four KM to the north? That's where my grandpa picked my mom and me up the night we were smuggled into Poland."

"Yes, that spot is still there, but you can't cross any more. There is a road up to it on the Ukrainian side, but they have a tall fence on the border now and the trees have all been cleared. If you want to drive up there, go ahead. I'll cover for you. It's a dead-end road. Check in here when you get back."

It took some time to drive up to the old crossing as the road was in poor repair.

"You said your grandpa had stuff for you to eat, right Daddy?" Gregory asked. "You must have been awful hungry."

"He had hot borsch and bread and butter with him in the cutter. We were so hungry! All I have to do is close my eyes and I can taste it again."

"That's the spot to the right, over there," Roger pointed. "That's where the Russian Lieutenant dropped us off and Grandpa picked us up. What a scary time it was."

Soon they were back to the border crossing and on their way.

They arrived in Novich late in the evening. The little village looked no different to Roger than it did the day they left. The innkeeper was happy to see them and booked them rooms for the night. Even though it was late, he insisted they join him for a big pot of borsch.

After an early breakfast, they met with the village administrator.

"I was fifteen when the Ukraine suffered the famine," the administrator said after looking at their visiting permits. "Fortunately for me, our family was in that part of the Ukraine where we had enough to eat. The older people in the village tell me horrible stories of suffering. From what they say, scores of villagers starved."

"My sister starved and my dad was shot for stealing a small bag of wheat," Roger interjected. "We've come to visit their graves."

"Yes, I see that by your papers. Years before my time, your families' old place was sold to your next door neighbors, the

Kowalchuks. From what I gathered, with none of your family here, it was sold for taxes. Many years ago the Kowalchuks tore down the old house, but they've taken excellent care of your little family graveyard. Do they know you're coming?"

"Yes, I wrote them a letter a month ago."

After talking to the administrator, Hartmann drove them to the old farmstead a kilometer or two out of town. Roger had phoned the collective farm overseer and asked for a tour of the old farm. The commune overseer, a stocky man in his early sixties, was there to meet them.

"I remember you," Roger said. "Your farm was next to ours."

"That's right. I remember you as a boy of seven or eight. That was before the famine. Look over there at the old cherry tree."

"Yes, I used to climb that tree and pick cherries into a pillow case I hung around my neck. Look kids. That's the cherry tree I told you about that I used to climb."

"Your Mom and Baba used to make wonderful cherry wine from those cherries," the overseer continued, "that I'll never forget. Then the famine came. It was so horrible I hardly want to think about it. I lost nearly all my family. Damn Stalin anyway," he muttered. "Only my oldest sister and I survived. There is lots of food to eat now though. Fortunately, we don't ever go to bed hungry."

After touring the old farmstead, they headed back into town and stopped at the Kowalchuks'. Both Fred and Lucy Kowalchuk came to the door. They were well into their seventies.

"Little Roger," Lucy cried. "I never thought I'd see you again in this world. God is so good to have spared your life. So many died here in this village, so many."

245

The town administrator dropped in to tell them that Roger and the group would be calling and Lucy had dinner about ready.

"Roger, you look so much like your dad," Fred said. "When you came walking down our sidewalk I did a double take, you resembled him so much. I buried your poor father the day after you and your mom were taken away in the army truck. Horrible days, horrible, horrible," he muttered.

"About three weeks later a man came to our door. He said he was from Poland and asked about your dad. I told him what had happened and he said that you and your mother had gotten to Poland safely. Is your mother still alive?"

"No, she didn't survive the war. Mom, my grandpa and I were all interred in slave labor camps when the Nazis occupied Poland. I'm the only one of the family to survive. Hartmann here was a very kind guard at that camp and got me transferred to a tank factory in Germany.

Neither Lucy nor Fred replied as tears slipped down their old wrinkled cheeks.

Lucy got up, went to the bedroom and returned with a small box. "These are a few old keepsakes we salvaged from your old house."

Roger shook his head in disbelief when he reached into the box and brought out the old ladle his mom used for making pickles.

"The man who brought news that you and your mother made it safely to Poland got us to gather up all the photos we could find in the house," Lucy continued. "Did you ever get those pictures?"

"Yes we did. He told us that Dad had been shot and that you people buried him in our yard. How did you manage to survive the famine?"

"Well, we saw it coming and had ten bags of wheat hidden in a secret place in our cellar," Fred replied. "When things got real tight we managed to sneak your folks a bag of wheat. I feel horrible that we didn't help more, but it got so no one dared to share their food. If the army caught you hoarding food or sharing it with your neighbors, it could mean instant death. They were such unbelievably cruel times. There never passes a day that I don't feel guilty that we lived through it and our neighbors didn't."

"Maybe we should talk about something more positive," Roger interjected. "I and my Polish cousin were finally awarded our Grandpa Jacob's estate. My step-grandma's brother had taken all of my grandpa's property and held it for many years. I would like to pay you folks for looking after the graves and if you could put up three more crosses for Mom, Grandpa Jacob and my step-grandma Freda, I'd appreciate that. I've made up five small metal plaques for all the crosses."

"The wife and I would be happy to do that for you, but we couldn't accept money for looking after the little cemetery. Remember, you were our neighbors and besides we have your old yard site. Caring for the graves is the least we can do."

After eating, Roger, Corrine, Hartmann, Elsie and the kids walked out to the grave sites. The picket fence was as Roger and his uncle had left it. The grass was newly mowed and the fence and crosses had just been painted.

They all gazed at the crosses in silence.

"It must make you really sad, Papa," Rosie said, breaking the spell. "Even I feel sad for your papa and baby sister."

Roger did not respond. He slowly dropped to his knees.

"My grandpa, my tato, my mama and my little sister Elena!" he cried. "I forgive. I forgive all those who caused me pain. God rest your soul Elena. God rest your soul Tato. God rest your soul Mama. God rest your soul Grandpa Jacob."

With Roger still on his knees, Corrine again began singing God Be With You Till We Meet Again. Rosie, like her mother had a beautiful voice and sang harmony.

As Roger slowly climbed to his feet, his face was aglow.

"It's unbelievable," he said. "I'd swear Papa, Mama, Elena, Grandpa Jacob and Freda are here with us. I've never experienced anything like this before, but it's so real. I can't see them, but I can feel their presence so strongly."

Corrine glanced up to an astonishing sight. There surrounding Roger were the spirits of his kinfolk, each with a hand on his shoulder.

"They are indeed, Dear," Corrine whispered. "They are indeed."

As quickly as the spirits appeared, they disappeared from Corrine's view. That no one else saw the spirits was no surprise to her. It had always been that way.

"Thank you so much for showing me the way, Mama," Roger whispered, looking upward. "I spent all those years controlled by anger and hate, but you finally got the message through to me. I now understand what you meant when you said:

WE MUST FORGIVE TO LIVE

CPSIA information can be obtained at www.ICGtesting.com
Printed in the USA
LVOW08s0020080414

380691LV00001B/32/P

9 781491 830338